THE GRAND CAN
100 DESTINATIONS

ARIZONA

TRAVEL GUIDE

DIANA L. MITCHELL

© **Copyright 2024 - All rights reserved.**

The content contained within this book may not be reproduced, duplicated or transmitted without direct written permission from the author or the publisher.

Under no circumstances will any blame or legal responsibility be held against the publisher, or author, for any damages, reparation, or monetary loss due to the information contained within this book, either directly or indirectly.

Legal Notice:

This book is copyright protected. It is only for personal use. You cannot amend, distribute, sell, use, quote or paraphrase any part, or the content within this book, without the consent of the author or publisher.

Disclaimer Notice:

Please note the information contained within this document is for educational and entertainment purposes only. All effort has been executed to present accurate, up to date, reliable, complete information. No warranties of any kind are declared or implied. Readers acknowledge that the author is not engaged in the rendering of legal, financial, medical or professional advice. The content within this book has been derived from various sources. Please consult a licensed professional before attempting any techniques outlined in this book.

By reading this document, the reader agrees that under no circumstances is the author responsible for any losses, direct or indirect, that are incurred as a result of the use of the information contained within this document, including, but not limited to, errors, omissions, or inaccuracies.

Cover image: © Funky Media sourced from canva.com

Table of Contents

Introduction 1
About Arizona 3
   Landscape of Arizona 3
      Desert Majesty: The Vast and Vibrant Sonoran 3
      Urban Oases and River Valleys 3
      Mountain Escapes and Pine Forests: The Northern Highlands 3
      The Grand Canyon: A Natural Wonder 4
      The Unique Charm of the Colorado River and Lake Havasu 4
      The Plateaus and Mesas 4
      In Conclusion 4
   The Flora and Fauna of Arizona 5
      Flora: A Desert Bloom 5
      Fauna: Diverse Desert Dwellers 6
      Preservation and Conservation Efforts 6
      In Conclusion 6
   The Climate of Arizona 7
      Seasonal Variations: A Landscape Transformed 7
      Regional Climate Differences 8
      Impact of Climate Change 8
      Preparing for Travel 8
      In Conclusion 9
   The History of Arizona 9
      Indigenous Heritage and Spanish Exploration 9
      Territorial Days and the Wild West 9
      Statehood and the 20th Century 10
      Historical Landmarks and Cultural Legacy 10
      In Conclusion 10

Northern Arizona ... 11

1. Montezuma Castle National Monument ... 11
2. Jerome ... 12
3. Tuzigoot National Monument ... 13
4. Sedona ... 14
5. Oak Creek Canyon ... 15
6. Slide Rock State Park ... 16
7. Meteor Crater ... 17
8. Walnut Canyon National Monument ... 18
9. Flagstaff ... 19
10. Bearizona Wildlife Park ... 20
11. Route 66 ... 21
12. Lava River Cave ... 22
13. Sunset Crater Volcano National Monument ... 23
14. Wupatki National Monument ... 24
15. Grand Canyon National Park ... 25
16. Havasu Falls ... 26
17. Vermilion Cliffs National Monument ... 27
18. Paria Canyon-Vermilion Cliffs Wilderness ... 28
19. Horseshoe Bend ... 29
20. Lake Powell ... 30
21. Antelope Canyon ... 31
22. Monument Valley ... 32
23. Navajo National Monument ... 33
24. Canyon de Chelly National Monument ... 34
25. Petrified Forest National Park ... 35

Southern Arizona ... 37

1. Ajo ... 37

2. Organ Pipe Cactus National Monument 38
3. Tohono O'odham Nation Cultural Center and Museum 39
4. Kitt Peak National Observatory 40
5. Tubac 41
6. Tumacácori National Historical Park 42
7. Patagonia Lake State Park 43
8. Ramsey Canyon Preserve 44
9. Bisbee 45
10. Tombstone 46
11. Chiricahua National Monument 47
12. Cochise Stronghold 48
13. Kartchner Caverns State Park 49
14. Elgin and Sonoita 50
15. Madera Canyon 51
16. Titan Missile Museum 52
17. Colossal Cave Mountain Park 53
18. Pima Air & Space Museum 54
19. Mission San Xavier del Bac 55
20. Tucson 56
21. Old Tucson Studios 57
22. Arizona-Sonora Desert Museum 58
23. Saguaro National Park 59
24. Catalina State Park 60
25. Mount Lemmon 61

Eastern Arizona 63
1. Rim Country Museum and Zane Grey Cabin 63
2. Mogollon Rim 64
3. Fool Hollow Lake Recreation Area 65

4.	Show Low	66
5.	Pinetop-Lakeside	67
6.	Kinishba Ruins	68
7.	Fort Apache Historic Park	69
8.	White Mountains	70
9.	Greer	71
10.	Butterfly Lodge Museum	72
11.	X Diamond Ranch	73
12.	Lyman Lake State Park	74
13.	Eagar	75
14.	Springerville Heritage Center	76
15.	Casa Malpais Archaeological Park	77
16.	Sipe White Mountain Wildlife Area	78
17.	Big Lake	79
18.	Coronado Trail Scenic Byway	80
19.	Alpine	81
20.	Apache-Sitgreaves National Forests	82
21.	Hannagan Meadow	83
22.	Blue Range Primitive Area	84
23.	Clifton and Morenci	85
24.	Roper Lake State Park	86
25.	Mount Graham International Observatory	87

Western Arizona 89

1.	Lake Mohave	89
2.	Black Mountains	90
3.	Route 66 Museum in Kingman	91
4.	Kingman	92
5.	Oatman	93

6.	Topock Gorge	94
7.	Lake Havasu City	95
8.	Sara Park (Special Activities and Recreation Area)	96
9.	Cattail Cove State Park	97
10.	Parker Dam	98
11.	Bill Williams River National Wildlife Refuge	99
12.	Aubrey Peak Wilderness	100
13.	Alamo Lake State Park	101
14.	Swansea Ghost Town	102
15.	Colorado River (Arizona Section)	103
16.	Buckskin Mountain State Park	104
17.	Desert Bar (Nellie E Saloon)	105
18.	Parker	106
19.	Quartzsite	107
20.	Wenden	108
21.	El Dorado Hot Springs	109
22.	Kofa National Wildlife Refuge	110
23.	Castle Dome Mines Museum & Ghost Town	111
24.	Yuma Proving Ground Heritage Center	112
25.	Yuma	113

Dear reader, thanks a lot for purchasing my book.

To help you plan your trip even more efficiently, I have included an interactive map powered by Google My Maps.

To access it, scan the QR code below.

Happy travelling!

A Note to Our Valued Readers

Thank you for choosing this travel guide as your companion for exploring the world.

I want to take a moment to address a concern you might have regarding the absence of photographs in this book.

As an independent author and publisher, I strive to deliver high-quality, informative content at an affordable price.

Including photographs in a printed book, however, presents significant challenges. Licensing high-quality images can be extremely costly, and unfortunately, I have no control over the print quality of images within the book.

Because these guides are printed and shipped by Amazon, I am unable to review the final print quality before they reach your hands.

So, rather than risk compromising your reading experience with subpar visuals, I've chosen to focus on providing detailed, insightful content that will help you make the most of your travels.

While this guide may not contain photos, it's packed with valuable information, insider tips, and recommendations to ensure you have an enriching and memorable journey.

Additionally, there's an interactive map powered by Google My Maps—an essential tool to help you plan your trip.

I encourage you to supplement your reading with online resources where you can find up-to-date images and visuals of the destinations covered in this guide.

I hope you find this book a helpful and inspiring resource as you embark on your next adventure.

Thank you for your understanding and support.

Safe travels,

Diana

Introduction

Welcome to *Arizona Travel Guide*, your quintessential guide to traversing the diverse and enchanting landscapes of the Grand Canyon State. From the awe-inspiring majesty of the Grand Canyon in the North to the serene beauty of the Sonoran Desert in the South, this guide is a comprehensive compendium for travelers seeking both the celebrated and the undiscovered jewels of Arizona.

Our adventure commences in Northern Arizona, a land imbued with natural wonders and cultural richness. Journey through the grandeur of the Grand Canyon National Park, where the vastness of the landscape humbles and inspires. Wander the mystical streets of Sedona, ablaze with its iconic red rocks, or delve into the ancient mysteries of Monument Valley. Experience the magic of Antelope Canyon's sculpted corridors and the grand spectacle of Horseshoe Bend. Each site presents a unique piece of Arizona's heart and history.

As we drift southwards, we encounter a kaleidoscope of desert marvels and historical intrigue. Uncover the hidden beauty of Saguaro National Park, home to the giant saguaros, an emblem of the American Southwest. Traverse the historic pathways of Tucson, brimming with cultural heritage, or step back in time in the legendary town of Tombstone. Southern Arizona is a harmonious blend of the old and new, offering experiences from the ethereal Kartchner Caverns to the vibrant streets of Bisbee.

Heading east, the narrative of Arizona continues to unfold in its verdant highlands and charming small towns. Eastern Arizona, a less-trodden path, reveals hidden gems like the White Mountains' pristine wilderness and the ancient ruins of the Casa Malpais Archaeological Park. This region is a haven for nature lovers and history buffs alike, with destinations like the Petrified Forest National Park and the quaint allure of Greer.

Our voyage then takes us to Western Arizona, where the Colorado River carves its way through the landscape, offering an oasis amidst the desert. Explore the recreational haven of Lake Havasu City, famous for its transplanted London Bridge, or immerse yourself in the riverfront charm of Parker. Western Arizona is a mosaic of natural beauty and human ingenuity, from the ghostly remnants of Oatman to the engineering marvel of the Parker Dam.

Arizona Travel Guide is not just a travel guide; it is a gateway to the soul of Arizona. Each of these 100 destinations has been meticulously chosen to present you with a journey that is as diverse as it is captivating. Pack your spirit of adventure, embrace your sense of wonder, and prepare to discover Arizona in a way you never imagined possible!

About Arizona

Landscape of Arizona

In *Arizona Travel Guide* we delve not just into the destinations but also the magnificent canvas upon which they are etched – the diverse and captivating landscape of Arizona. This chapter explores the varied terrains and natural wonders that make the Grand Canyon State a vivid showcase of the American Southwest's natural splendor.

Desert Majesty: The Vast and Vibrant Sonoran

Southern Arizona is renowned for the Sonoran Desert's sprawling landscape. From the towering Saguaro cacti standing sentinel over the valley to the colorful sunsets painting the skies of Tucson, this region is a symphony of earth and sky. The desert, with its unique flora and fauna, shapes the culture and lifestyle of the communities that call it home. It's a land where ancient traditions blend seamlessly with modern living.

Urban Oases and River Valleys

The urban centers of Phoenix and Scottsdale are artfully mingled with natural beauty. Spaces like the Desert Botanical Garden and Papago Park offer lush, green sanctuaries amidst the urban sprawl. The Salt River winds through these cities, providing a vital lifeline and a picturesque setting for hiking, birdwatching, and watersports.

Mountain Escapes and Pine Forests: The Northern Highlands

Northern Arizona is characterized by its dramatic elevation changes, from deep canyons to towering peaks. This region boasts a landscape of pine forests, serene meadows, and hidden lakes. The San Francisco Peaks and the charming town of Flagstaff offer a respite from the desert heat, with snow-capped winters and cool summers. The highlands are a tapestry of outdoor adventures and tranquil retreats.

The Grand Canyon: A Natural Wonder

The crown jewel of Arizona's landscape, the Grand Canyon, is an unparalleled spectacle. Stretching over vast distances, its layered rocks tell the story of geological epochs. The canyon, with its immense size and awe-inspiring beauty, is a destination unto itself, offering breathtaking views, challenging hikes, and a profound sense of nature's majesty.

The Unique Charm of the Colorado River and Lake Havasu

Western Arizona is defined by the life-giving waters of the Colorado River and Lake Havasu. This region is a paradise for water enthusiasts, with its sprawling lakes and rivers set against desert backdrops. Lake Havasu City, with its famous London Bridge, and the serene shores of the Colorado River offer a blend of recreational activities and scenic beauty.

The Plateaus and Mesas

Arizona's landscape is also marked by its high plateaus and dramatic mesas, shaping the skyline with their striking formations. Regions like the Monument Valley and the Painted Desert showcase a panorama of colors and shapes, offering a glimpse into the state's geological past and the rich Native American heritage.

In Conclusion

The landscape of Arizona is as diverse as its cultural tapestry. From sun-drenched deserts to snow-laden mountain peaks, from bustling city parks to the tranquil expanse of the Grand Canyon, the state's natural beauty offers a myriad of experiences for every traveler. As you explore these landscapes, remember that they are not just a backdrop but an integral part of Arizona's enchanting story.

The Flora and Fauna of Arizona

In *Arizona Travel Guide*, we venture beyond the vibrant towns and cities to explore the rich tapestry of natural life that Arizona harbors. This chapter is dedicated to the diverse flora and fauna that grace the landscapes of the Grand Canyon State, offering a glimpse into the vibrant ecosystems thriving in this varied region.

Flora: A Desert Bloom

Arizona's flora is a testament to nature's resilience, flourishing across its varied geography and climate zones. From the lush riparian areas to the arid deserts and the high mountain forests, each area showcases its own unique plant life.

Desert Vegetation: In the Sonoran Desert, hardy cacti like the iconic Saguaro, cholla, and prickly pear dominate. Desert wildflowers, such as the vibrant Mexican poppy and desert marigold, add bursts of color.

Mountain Flora: Higher altitudes, like the San Francisco Peaks, host a different flora, including Ponderosa pines, Douglas firs, and aspens. These forests offer a stark contrast to the desert landscapes and are known for their spectacular fall colors.

Riparian Areas: Arizona's rivers and streams support lush vegetation, including cottonwoods, willows, and mesquite. These areas are crucial for wildlife and serve as important ecological corridors in the arid landscape.

Unique Species: Arizona is home to unique and endemic plant species like the Arizona Cypress and the Joshua tree. The state also protects several endangered plant species within its parks and preserves.

Fauna: Diverse Desert Dwellers

The animal life in Arizona is as varied as its flora, ranging from the iconic desert dwellers to the mountain inhabitants.

Desert Wildlife: The Sonoran Desert is teeming with life, including mammals like the javelina, coyote, and desert bighorn sheep. The Gila monster and a variety of rattlesnakes are among the notable reptiles.

Birds: Arizona is a paradise for birdwatchers. The state is renowned for its hummingbirds and birds of prey, including the majestic bald eagle and peregrine falcon. The riparian areas are crucial for migratory birds.

Mountain Fauna: In the higher elevations, species like the elk, black bear, and Mexican gray wolf roam. The White Mountains and other high-altitude areas offer a habitat for these larger mammals.

Insects and Amphibians: The diverse insect life, including the iconic monarch butterfly, plays a vital role in pollination. Amphibians like the Sonoran desert toad are unique to Arizona's ecosystems.

Preservation and Conservation Efforts

Arizona is dedicated to preserving its natural heritage. Various conservation programs and protected areas, such as the Saguaro National Park and the Arizona-Sonora Desert Museum, work towards the survival of many species and their habitats. Initiatives like the Arizona Endangered Species Act safeguard the state's rich biodiversity.

In Conclusion

The flora and fauna of Arizona are central to the state's identity and appeal. They bring life and beauty to the landscape and are crucial for ecological balance. As you journey through Arizona, take time to appreciate the natural splendor and biodiversity that the Grand Canyon State offers. It's a journey through not just the physical landscape but also the living tapestry that forms an integral part of Arizona's story.

In *Arizona Travel Guide*, the climate is not just a backdrop but a dynamic character that shapes the experiences at each destination. This chapter dives into the climate of Arizona, shedding light on how it influences the landscapes, flora, fauna, and the overall travel experience across the state.

The Climate of Arizona

Seasonal Variations: A Landscape Transformed

Arizona's climate varies dramatically, from arid desert conditions to alpine weather in the high mountains, offering a diverse range of experiences throughout the year.

Spring (March to May): This season brings a mild and pleasant climate, especially in the desert regions. Wildflowers bloom across the landscape, painting the desert in vibrant colors. In the mountains, the snow begins to melt, revealing lush greenery.

Summer (June to August): Summers in Arizona are hot, particularly in the lower desert areas where temperatures can soar. However, the higher elevations offer a cooler escape, with pleasant temperatures ideal for hiking and outdoor activities. Monsoon season starts in late summer, bringing refreshing rains and dramatic thunderstorms.

Fall (September to November): Autumn sees a gradual cooling, especially pleasant in the desert. The foliage in the higher regions turns into a display of golds and reds. The lower temperatures and clear skies make this an ideal time for exploring both the desert and mountain regions.

Winter (December to February): Winters vary greatly. In the desert, days are mild and sunny, perfect for outdoor activities, while nights can be cool. In contrast, the highlands, including areas like the White Mountains, receive snowfall, creating opportunities for winter sports like skiing and snowshoeing.

Regional Climate Differences

The climate in Arizona varies significantly across regions:

Desert Areas: These regions experience extremely hot summers and mild winters. Rain is scarce, except during the monsoon season in late summer.

Mountainous Areas: Higher altitudes, such as the San Francisco Peaks, experience cooler temperatures year-round, with cold winters that bring snow.

Impact of Climate Change

Arizona is witnessing the impacts of climate change, with increasing temperatures, changing precipitation patterns, and more intense monsoon seasons. These changes are affecting the natural environment and are a focus of ongoing study and adaptation efforts.

Preparing for Travel

When planning a visit to Arizona, consider the dramatic climate variations:

Spring and Fall: Light clothing for daytime, with layers for cooler evenings, especially in the desert.

Summer: Lightweight, breathable attire is essential for the desert heat, along with hats and sunscreen. In the mountains, pack for mild and cooler temperatures.

Winter: Warm clothing for the highlands, including coats and snow gear for winter sports. Desert areas require lighter clothing but include layers for cooler evenings.

In Conclusion

The climate of Arizona offers a dynamic and diverse experience, from the sun-drenched deserts to the snow-capped peaks. Whether you're exploring the Grand Canyon under the summer sun, witnessing the desert bloom in spring, or enjoying winter sports in the northern highlands, understanding the climate is key to a fulfilling Arizona adventure.

The History of Arizona

In *Arizona Travel Guide*, the history of Arizona is not just a backdrop but a fundamental aspect of the state's identity. This chapter invites you on a journey through time, exploring the rich historical tapestry that has shaped Arizona into the diverse and vibrant state it is today.

Indigenous Heritage and Spanish Exploration

Long before European exploration, Arizona was home to various Native American tribes, including the Navajo, Hopi, and Apache. Their profound connection to the land and enduring cultures have significantly impacted the state's heritage.

The first European to arrive in the region was Spanish explorer Marcos de Niza in 1539, followed by Coronado in search of the mythical Seven Cities of Gold. These early explorations paved the way for subsequent Spanish settlements and missions, leaving a lasting influence on the region's culture and architecture.

Territorial Days and the Wild West

Arizona's history is deeply rooted in the lore of the Wild West. The mid-19th century brought American prospectors, leading to the iconic Gold Rush era. Towns like Tombstone and Oatman, famous for their gunfights and mining tales, capture the spirit of this period.

In 1863, Arizona became a separate territory, distinct from New Mexico, marking a new chapter in its development. The latter half of the 19th century saw significant growth, with the establishment of railroads and increased mining activity.

Statehood and the 20th Century

Arizona became the 48th state of the United States in 1912. The 20th century saw dramatic changes, with the growth of cities like Phoenix and Tucson. During World War II, Arizona was a crucial training ground for the military, and the post-war period brought rapid economic and demographic growth.

The state has also been a center for Native American rights movements, reflecting its ongoing commitment to respecting and preserving its indigenous cultures.

Historical Landmarks and Cultural Legacy

Arizona is dotted with historical landmarks that tell the story of its past. The missions of Tumacácori and San Xavier del Bac, the preserved cliff dwellings at Montezuma Castle, and the frontier tales of the OK Corral in Tombstone are vivid portals into history.

In Conclusion

Understanding the history of Arizona is key to appreciating its present. From its indigenous heritage to its role in the Old West, and its ongoing legacy of cultural diversity and growth, Arizona's history is a testament to the resilience and spirit of its people. As you explore the destinations in this guide, take a moment to reflect on the historical significance of each location and how it has contributed to the tapestry that is Arizona today.

Northern Arizona

1. Montezuma Castle National Monument

Montezuma Castle National Monument, located near Camp Verde, Arizona, is a remarkable site that preserves one of the best-preserved cliff dwellings in North America. Constructed by the Sinagua people, a pre-Columbian culture that thrived in the region from approximately 1100 to 1425 AD, this ancient structure stands as a testament to the ingenuity and resourcefulness of its builders. Despite its name, the site has no connection to the Aztec emperor Montezuma; early European settlers mistakenly attributed the structure to the Aztecs, and the name has endured.

The main feature of Montezuma Castle is a striking five-story, 20-room dwelling built into a limestone cliff face about 90 feet above the ground. This strategic location provided the Sinagua people with protection from floods and invaders while offering a commanding view of the surrounding Verde Valley. The cliff dwelling, constructed using limestone and mortar, is an impressive feat of engineering that demonstrates the Sinagua's deep understanding of their environment and architectural skills. Although visitors are no longer allowed to enter the structure to preserve it, they can view it from a distance along well-maintained trails.

The visitor center at Montezuma Castle National Monument provides valuable context about the Sinagua culture and the history of the site. Exhibits showcase artifacts such as pottery, tools, and woven materials, giving insight into the daily lives of the people who once inhabited the area. Rangers and interpretive displays help visitors understand how the Sinagua adapted to the harsh desert environment and sustained their community through farming, hunting, and trade.

In addition to Montezuma Castle, the monument also includes Montezuma Well, a natural limestone sinkhole that served as a crucial water source for the Sinagua and other indigenous cultures. The well's unique ecosystem and fascinating irrigation canals are worth exploring, adding to the overall experience of visiting the monument.

Montezuma Castle National Monument offers a glimpse into a bygone era, inviting visitors to reflect on the resilience and ingenuity of the people who once made their home in this arid, yet beautiful landscape.

2. Jerome

Nestled on the side of Cleopatra Hill in central Arizona, Jerome is a fascinating and picturesque town known for its colorful history and unique blend of art, mining heritage, and ghostly legends. Once a thriving mining town dubbed the "Wickedest Town in the West," Jerome has transformed into a lively tourist destination and artist haven, while still preserving the remnants of its rich past.

Founded in the late 19th century, Jerome quickly grew into one of Arizona's largest and wealthiest towns, thanks to the discovery of vast copper deposits. At its peak in the 1920s, the town had a population of over 15,000 people, attracting miners, prospectors, and adventurers from all over the country. However, when the copper mines began to close in the mid-20th century, Jerome's population dwindled to just a handful of residents, and the town nearly became a ghost town. In the 1960s and 70s, artists and craftspeople started moving in, revitalizing Jerome and turning it into the vibrant community it is today.

Visitors to Jerome can explore its rich mining history by visiting the Jerome State Historic Park and the Douglas Mansion, a museum dedicated to the town's past. The museum features fascinating exhibits, including mining equipment, historic photographs, and detailed accounts of the town's heyday. For an even more immersive experience, the Gold King Mine and Ghost Town provide a glimpse into the gritty, wild days of mining, with old mining machinery, vintage vehicles, and even a working sawmill.

Jerome's winding streets are lined with art galleries, boutique shops, and cozy cafes, offering a laid-back atmosphere and stunning views of the Verde Valley below. The town's bohemian spirit is palpable, and visitors will find a wide range of unique artwork and handcrafted goods created by local artists. Jerome is also known for its haunted reputation, and ghost tours are a popular activity, taking guests through historic buildings like the Jerome Grand Hotel, which is said to be one of the most haunted places in Arizona.

With its combination of history, art, and a touch of the supernatural, Jerome is a captivating destination that offers something for everyone. The town's blend of the Old West and modern creativity makes it a memorable stop for anyone exploring Arizona's rich cultural landscape.

3. Tuzigoot National Monument

Tuzigoot National Monument, located near Clarkdale, Arizona, is a significant archaeological site that preserves the remnants of a large Sinagua pueblo. The Sinagua people, who flourished in the Verde Valley between the 12th and 15th centuries, constructed this impressive hilltop settlement, which offers a fascinating glimpse into the lives and culture of an ancient civilization. The name "Tuzigoot," derived from the Apache word for "crooked water," refers to the winding course of the nearby Verde River.

The Tuzigoot pueblo consists of a series of interconnected rooms and structures built atop a limestone ridge, offering panoramic views of the surrounding valley and river. At its peak, the pueblo had over 110 rooms, including storage areas, living quarters, and communal spaces. The structures were constructed using local limestone and sandstone, and the walls were skillfully shaped with mortar, reflecting the Sinagua's resourcefulness and craftsmanship. Unlike some cliff dwellings, Tuzigoot was a free-standing complex, designed to take advantage of the ridge's natural elevation for defense and visibility.

Visitors to Tuzigoot National Monument can walk through the partially reconstructed ruins and climb to the top of the pueblo, where breathtaking views of the landscape await. Interpretive trails and signage provide information about the Sinagua people's way of life, including their agricultural practices, trade networks, and cultural traditions. The site's visitor center houses a small but informative museum with exhibits showcasing artifacts such as pottery, stone tools, and woven materials, all of which illustrate the daily activities and artistic expression of the Sinagua.

Tuzigoot National Monument not only offers an opportunity to learn about the history and culture of the Sinagua but also highlights the natural beauty of the Verde Valley. The surrounding area is a haven for birdwatching and wildlife observation, with the river and nearby wetlands providing a rich habitat for a variety of species. The monument is an excellent destination for those interested in archaeology, Native American history, and the serene, rugged beauty of the Southwest.

Whether you're exploring the ruins, admiring the views, or learning about the Sinagua culture, Tuzigoot National Monument offers a captivating and educational experience that transports visitors back in time to an era when the Verde Valley was a thriving cultural hub.

4. Sedona

Nestled amidst the striking red sandstone formations of the American Southwest, is a destination that effortlessly blends natural beauty, spiritual wellness, and artistic flair.

The unique geological features that define Sedona's landscape were formed by millions of years of sedimentation and erosion. These red and orange sandstone formations glow brilliantly under the Arizona sun, creating a stunning visual spectacle. The most famous of these formations include Cathedral Rock, Bell Rock, and Courthouse Butte, each holding a special place in the local lore and attracting hikers, photographers, and nature enthusiasts from around the world.

Sedona's reputation as a spiritual center is another key aspect of its allure. The region is considered a hotspot for 'vortexes' - specific areas that are believed to be energy centers conducive to healing, meditation, and self-exploration. These vortexes have made Sedona a pilgrimage site for New Age enthusiasts. Whether or not one subscribes to the vortex theories, there's no denying the sense of peace and awe that pervades Sedona's landscape.

The city's artistic community is vibrant and thriving. Sedona has long been a haven for artists inspired by its natural beauty and mystical qualities. This is reflected in the numerous art galleries and studios that dot the city, showcasing everything from Southwestern landscapes to contemporary abstract works. The Sedona Arts Festival and other cultural events offer a platform for artists to display their work and for visitors to immerse themselves in the local art scene.

Outdoor activities in Sedona are plentiful and cater to all levels of adventure. The numerous hiking and biking trails provide a way to intimately experience the beauty of the red rocks. Jeep tours, hot air balloon rides, and horseback riding offer alternative and thrilling ways to explore the rugged landscape. For those seeking a more relaxed experience, the Oak Creek Canyon, with its serene creek and natural pools, is perfect for picnicking and swimming.

Sedona is not just about nature and spirituality; it also offers a range of dining and shopping experiences. The city boasts an array of restaurants serving everything from sophisticated gourmet dishes to hearty Southwestern cuisine. Shops and boutiques offer unique local crafts, jewelry, and art, making Sedona a unique shopping destination.

5. Oak Creek Canyon

Oak Creek Canyon, a scenic river gorge located in northern Arizona, is often described as a smaller cousin of the Grand Canyon. This breathtakingly beautiful canyon, stretching approximately 12 miles and ranging in depth from 800 to 2,000 feet, is carved by Oak Creek, a tributary of the Verde River. The canyon is known for its stunning red rock walls, lush riparian vegetation, and diverse wildlife.

The drive through Oak Creek Canyon, via State Route 89A between Sedona and Flagstaff, is considered one of the most scenic drives in America. The winding road descends through the canyon, offering views of the towering cliffs, dense greenery, and the meandering creek below.

The canyon is a popular destination for outdoor activities such as hiking, camping, fishing, and swimming. Slide Rock State Park, located within the canyon, is famous for its natural water slides and swimming holes, making it a perfect spot for families and nature enthusiasts.

Hiking trails in Oak Creek Canyon range from easy walks along the creek to more challenging treks up the canyon walls. The West Fork Trail, one of the most popular hikes in the area, takes visitors through lush forests, over streams, and offers spectacular views of the canyon.

In addition to its natural beauty, Oak Creek Canyon is also rich in history and culture. The area has been inhabited for thousands of years, first by Native American tribes and later by settlers who established orchards and homesteads in the fertile valley.

Oak Creek Canyon is not just a natural wonder but also a place of relaxation and rejuvenation. The serene beauty of the creek, the shade of the sycamore and cottonwood trees, and the majestic red rocks create a peaceful and inviting atmosphere. Whether you're seeking adventure or a quiet retreat in nature, Oak Creek Canyon provides an unforgettable experience in one of Arizona's most picturesque settings.

6. Slide Rock State Park

Slide Rock State Park, a natural wonder and popular outdoor destination in Arizona, is nestled in the heart of Oak Creek Canyon, just north of Sedona. Spanning 43 acres, this park is named after its famous Slide Rock, a smooth, slippery chute carved into the red sandstone, creating a natural water slide. The park, originally the Pendley Homestead, is not only a testament to the unique geological features of the region but also to the rich agricultural history of Oak Creek Canyon.

The slide itself is a 30-foot-long slick natural water slide formed by the slippery bed of Oak Creek. Visitors flock to the park to glide down the slide into the refreshing water below, especially during the hot summer months. The creek extends beyond the slide, offering numerous swimming holes and sunbathing spots along its banks. Surrounded by towering red rocks and lush vegetation, the natural waters of Slide Rock make it one of the most picturesque swimming spots in Arizona.

However, Slide Rock State Park offers more than just aquatic fun. It is a piece of living history, showcasing the early 20th-century ingenuity in agriculture. The park was originally an apple orchard, established by Frank L. Pendley in 1912, who secured water rights and developed an innovative irrigation system which is still in use today. Visitors can explore the historic Pendley Homestead, the apple packing barn, and the old cabins to get a glimpse into the early settler life.

The park's unique location in Oak Creek Canyon provides it with a diverse range of flora and fauna. The creek supports a riparian habitat with various species of trees, shrubs, and wildlife. Birdwatchers and nature enthusiasts can enjoy the sight of native birds and the occasional wildlife sightings along the creek.

For those interested in hiking, Slide Rock State Park offers several short trails. These trails wind through the apple orchards, along the creek, and up to the higher grounds, offering stunning views of the canyon. The Pendley Homestead Trail, for instance, is an easy, educational trail that provides insights into the history of the park.

Slide Rock State Park is not only a place for relaxation and recreation but also an area of outstanding natural beauty and historical significance. It represents the harmonious blend of natural and human history, providing a unique outdoor experience for visitors.

7. Meteor Crater

Meteor Crater, located near Winslow in northern Arizona, is one of the best-preserved meteorite impact sites on Earth. Formed approximately 50,000 years ago during the Pleistocene epoch, this iconic natural landmark stands as a testament to the incredible forces of nature. The crater measures about 3,900 feet (1,200 meters) in diameter and 560 feet (170 meters) deep, with a rim that rises 148 feet (45 meters) above the surrounding desert plains. Its vast scale makes it a must-see destination for geology enthusiasts, astronomers, and curious travelers alike.

The crater was created when a nickel-iron meteorite, estimated to be about 150 feet (50 meters) wide and weighing several hundred thousand tons, slammed into the Earth at a speed of roughly 26,000 miles per hour (42,000 kilometers per hour). The impact released energy equivalent to about 10 megatons of TNT, instantly creating the massive cavity and scattering debris over several miles.

For years, the origin of Meteor Crater was debated. Initially, scientists speculated that it was volcanic in nature. However, in the early 20th century, Daniel Barringer, a mining engineer and geologist, championed the idea that it was caused by a meteorite impact. His groundbreaking work laid the foundation for modern impact crater studies, and the site is now officially named the Barringer Crater in his honor.

Today, Meteor Crater is privately owned and operated by the Barringer family. The site features a visitor center with interactive exhibits, a museum, and a theater showcasing educational films about the crater's formation and its scientific significance. Visitors can explore the rim on guided tours, marvel at fragments of the meteorite on display, and enjoy panoramic views of the Arizona desert.

As a natural laboratory for studying impact craters, Meteor Crater continues to attract researchers from around the globe. Its stark beauty and rich history make it a fascinating destination that offers a glimpse into the dynamic forces that have shaped our planet.

8. Walnut Canyon National Monument

Walnut Canyon National Monument, located near Flagstaff in Northern Arizona, is a hidden gem that offers a remarkable glimpse into the lives of the ancient peoples who once inhabited this region. This national monument, rich in both natural beauty and historical significance, encompasses a striking canyon with sheer walls and distinctive geological formations.

The main draw of Walnut Canyon is the remarkable series of cliff dwellings, built by the Sinagua people around 700 years ago. These dwellings, nestled along the limestone cliffs of the canyon, are a testament to the ingenuity and resilience of their builders. The Sinagua were a pre-Columbian culture known for their agricultural skills, craftsmanship, and trade networks, which extended far across the Southwest.

Visitors to Walnut Canyon can explore the Island Trail, a one-mile loop that descends into the canyon and offers up-close views of these ancient dwellings. As you walk along this trail, you're not just seeing the remnants of ancient homes; you're walking through a slice of human history. The trail also provides stunning views of the canyon itself, with its diverse array of flora, including ponderosa pines and a variety of shrubs and wildflowers.

The Rim Trail, another option for visitors, offers a less strenuous experience with overlooks of the canyon and the surrounding landscape. It's an excellent choice for those who prefer an easier walk or for visitors short on time. Along both trails, interpretive signs provide context about the Sinagua people and the diverse ecosystems within the canyon.

Walnut Canyon National Monument is not only a place of historical and archaeological importance; it's also a site of natural splendor. The canyon, with its rich array of plant and animal life, offers a peaceful retreat into nature. Birdwatchers and nature enthusiasts will find much to appreciate, from the soaring birds of prey overhead to the small creatures that make their home in this diverse habitat.

In conclusion, Walnut Canyon National Monument offers a unique blend of natural beauty and a deep connection to the past. It stands as a reminder of the ancient people who once thrived in the American Southwest and a testament to the enduring allure of Arizona's natural landscapes.

9. Flagstaff

Nestled in the shadows of the San Francisco Peaks and surrounded by the largest ponderosa pine forest in North America, is a vibrant and eclectic city that blends outdoor adventure with cultural richness. Located on the iconic Route 66, this mountain town is a gateway to the wonders of the American Southwest, including the Grand Canyon, Sedona's red rocks, and the Native American reservations.

At an elevation of 7,000 feet, Flagstaff enjoys a unique high-altitude climate that contrasts sharply with the arid deserts typically associated with Arizona. This elevation brings cool summers and snowy winters, making it a year-round destination for outdoor enthusiasts. In summer, it's a haven for hikers, mountain bikers, and campers, while winter draws skiers and snowboarders to the nearby Arizona Snowbowl.

Flagstaff's downtown area is a lively hub with a distinct small-town charm. Historic buildings line the streets, housing a variety of local boutiques, restaurants, and breweries. The city's cultural scene is vibrant, with numerous galleries, theaters, and music venues showcasing local and national talent. The First Friday Art Walk, a monthly event, celebrates this artistic vitality, turning the downtown area into a festive display of art, music, and community.

The city is also a center of education and research, home to Northern Arizona University and the Lowell Observatory. The observatory, one of the oldest in the United States, is where Pluto was discovered in 1930. It remains an active research center and a popular attraction, offering public telescope viewing and educational programs that bring the wonders of the universe closer to earth.

Flagstaff's rich cultural heritage is deeply intertwined with the Native American tribes of the region. The Museum of Northern Arizona and the Riordan Mansion State Historic Park provide insights into the area's history and cultures, from its indigenous roots to its pioneer days.

Environmental conservation is a significant focus in Flagstaff. The city is surrounded by natural beauty, from the Coconino National Forest to the volcanic fields of Sunset Crater Volcano National Monument. These natural wonders are not only a source of recreation but also a reminder of the importance of preserving our natural environment.

10. Bearizona Wildlife Park

Bearizona Wildlife Park, located in Williams, Arizona, is a unique and family-friendly wildlife adventure that offers visitors an up-close and personal experience with North American animals in their natural habitats. Spanning over 160 acres, Bearizona combines the thrill of a drive-through safari with a traditional walk-through wildlife exhibit, making it an unforgettable destination for animal lovers of all ages.

The park's main attraction is the drive-through section, where visitors can drive their own vehicles along a scenic, three-mile route through diverse habitats. As you make your way through the park, you'll encounter an array of free-roaming animals, including black bears, bison, wolves, mountain goats, elk, and more. The animals are separated into different enclosures to ensure safety while providing an environment that closely resembles their natural homes. Seeing these majestic creatures in a setting that allows them to roam freely is a truly awe-inspiring experience.

After the drive-through adventure, visitors can explore Fort Bearizona, the walk-through portion of the park. Here, you'll find a variety of smaller animal exhibits, including playful otters, mischievous raccoons, and adorable foxes. Fort Bearizona also features a petting zoo where children can interact with friendly farm animals, as well as daily animal shows and educational presentations that highlight conservation efforts and animal behavior. The Birds of Prey show is a must-see, showcasing the incredible talents of raptors as they soar overhead.

Bearizona is committed to wildlife conservation and education, and the park provides opportunities for visitors to learn about the animals and the importance of preserving their habitats. The park's staff works diligently to ensure that the animals receive top-notch care and that visitors have a meaningful and respectful experience.

Located just off historic Route 66, Bearizona Wildlife Park is a fantastic stop for families, wildlife enthusiasts, and travelers exploring northern Arizona. With its combination of thrilling wildlife encounters and engaging educational programs, Bearizona offers a one-of-a-kind experience that highlights the beauty and diversity of North American wildlife.

11. Route 66

Route 66, often referred to as the "Mother Road," is one of the most iconic highways in American history. Stretching nearly 2,500 miles from Chicago, Illinois, to Santa Monica, California, this legendary road was established in 1926 and became a symbol of freedom and adventure for countless travelers. Route 66 played a vital role in the development of the American West and remains a nostalgic journey through time, with vintage diners, quirky roadside attractions, and scenic landscapes that capture the spirit of a bygone era.

Arizona hosts some of the most picturesque and memorable segments of Route 66, with its winding roads taking travelers through charming towns, stunning deserts, and breathtaking mountain vistas. Towns like Williams, Flagstaff, and Kingman are filled with history and character, offering visitors a taste of what life was like during the heyday of this legendary highway. Williams, known as the "Gateway to the Grand Canyon," is a particularly popular stop, complete with retro diners, neon signs, and classic motels that transport visitors back to the 1950s.

One of the most iconic attractions along Arizona's stretch of Route 66 is the Petrified Forest National Park, where travelers can explore ancient fossilized trees and colorful badlands. Other must-see stops include the famous Hackberry General Store, which is filled with Route 66 memorabilia and nostalgic souvenirs, and Seligman, a town that proudly claims to be the "Birthplace of Route 66" and is packed with classic cars, historic buildings, and vintage Americana.

Route 66 is more than just a highway; it's a journey that tells the story of America's past, from the Dust Bowl migrations of the 1930s to the rise of car culture in the 1950s. It continues to attract road trip enthusiasts from around the world who are eager to experience the romance and adventure of this historic route. With its rich history, stunning scenery, and enduring appeal, Route 66 remains a symbol of the American spirit and a must-do adventure for travelers seeking to explore the heart of the country.

12. Lava River Cave

Lava River Cave, located in the Coconino National Forest near Flagstaff, Arizona, is an extraordinary natural wonder that offers a thrilling subterranean adventure. Formed roughly 700,000 years ago by a volcanic eruption, this mile-long lava tube was created when molten lava flowed underground, leaving behind a massive, hollow tunnel as the outer layers cooled and solidified. Today, Lava River Cave provides a unique opportunity for visitors to explore the geological forces that have shaped the region's landscape.

Descending into Lava River Cave is like stepping into another world. The entrance, a rocky descent through a collapsed section of the cave, leads visitors into a dark and mysterious underground realm. Temperatures inside the cave remain a cool 40 degrees Fahrenheit year-round, so warm clothing and sturdy footwear are essential. Visitors are also advised to bring multiple sources of light, such as flashlights or headlamps, as the cave is completely unlit and pitch dark.

As you make your way through the tunnel, you'll encounter a variety of fascinating geological features. The cave's walls and ceiling are adorned with ripples and lava stalactites, remnants of the molten lava that once flowed through the area. The floor can be uneven, with large boulders and sections of hardened lava flow, adding to the sense of adventure as you navigate the cave's twists and turns. In some areas, the tunnel opens up into spacious chambers, while in others, it narrows to low passages that require careful maneuvering.

Exploring Lava River Cave is a thrilling experience for those with a sense of adventure and an interest in geology. The cave is a testament to the volcanic activity that shaped northern Arizona's landscape, and it offers a unique opportunity to see the inner workings of a lava tube up close. However, it's important to respect the cave's fragile ecosystem and practice Leave No Trace principles to preserve this natural wonder for future generations.

Whether you're a seasoned caver or a first-time explorer, Lava River Cave provides an unforgettable experience. The combination of eerie darkness, ancient geological formations, and the thrill of discovery makes it a must-visit destination for anyone exploring the wonders of the Coconino National Forest.

13. Sunset Crater Volcano National Monument

Sunset Crater Volcano National Monument, situated just north of Flagstaff in Arizona, offers a fascinating look into the raw power of volcanic activity and its impact on the surrounding landscape. This unique national monument preserves the youngest and best-preserved volcanic field in the contiguous United States, with its centerpiece being the stunning Sunset Crater. The crater, formed by a series of eruptions that occurred around 1085 AD, is a stark reminder of the dynamic forces shaping our planet.

The eruption of Sunset Crater dramatically altered the landscape, covering the surrounding area with lava flows and ash, changing the ecosystem and impacting the local communities living here centuries ago. Today, the monument stands as a testament to nature's incredible power to both destroy and create. The volcanic activity enriched the soil, allowing a diverse range of plant life to flourish in the area over time.

Sunset Crater itself is an impressive sight, with its rim and sides colored in shades of red and orange, resembling a sunset – a feature that gives the volcano its name. The contrasting colors of the cinder cone, made up of fragments of lava, create a visually striking landscape that captivates visitors.

Visitors to the monument can explore a variety of trails, offering different perspectives and experiences of the volcanic landscape. The Lava Flow Trail is a one-mile loop that winds through the rugged terrain of hardened lava and volcanic ash, providing an up-close view of the diverse geological features. For those seeking a panoramic view, the Cinder Hills Overlook offers a breathtaking vista of the entire volcanic field.

In addition to its geological wonders, Sunset Crater Volcano National Monument provides a habitat for a variety of wildlife. The area's flora and fauna have adapted to the harsh volcanic environment, making it an interesting place for nature observation and photography.

The monument also offers educational opportunities, with interpretive displays and ranger-led programs that delve into the geological history of the area, as well as the impact of the eruption on the ancient Puebloan people who once inhabited the region.

14. Wupatki National Monument

Wupatki National Monument, a testament to ancient human ingenuity and resilience, is located in Northern Arizona, just north of Flagstaff. Encompassing over 35,000 acres, this site is rich in archaeological and cultural significance, offering a window into the lives of the Ancient Pueblo People who once inhabited this land.

The name 'Wupatki' means 'Tall House' in the Hopi language, aptly describing the multistoried ruins that are the monument's main attraction. The landscape here is diverse, featuring vast grasslands, scattered forests, and striking red rock formations, providing a stark contrast to the nearby volcanic fields.

The monument's most significant structure, Wupatki Pueblo, was one of the largest communities in the area, containing over 100 rooms. This grand edifice highlights the advanced masonry skills of its builders and is believed to have served as an important ceremonial and trading center. The nearby Wukoki and Lomaki Pueblos, while smaller, offer further insight into the architectural styles and living conditions of the time.

One of Wupatki's unique features is its blowhole, a geological phenomenon that acts as a natural air vent, further adding to the mystique of the area. Another intriguing site is the Wupatki Ball Court, suggesting a connection between the Puebloan peoples and the ancient civilizations of Mesoamerica.

Wupatki National Monument is not just a collection of ruins; it is a place where visitors can connect with the past. The site's interpretive trails and guided tours provide a comprehensive understanding of the region's ancient cultures, their daily lives, agricultural practices, and commerce.

15. Grand Canyon National Park

Grand Canyon National Park, an iconic symbol of natural wonder and geological magnificence, stands as one of the most awe-inspiring destinations in the world. Located in Northern Arizona, the park covers an area of over 1.2 million acres, encompassing vast and varied landscapes shaped over millions of years. This majestic canyon, carved by the Colorado River, offers a spectacular display of intricate designs, vibrant colors, and immense scale, capturing the imagination of visitors from all corners of the globe.

The Grand Canyon's immense size, with an average depth of over a mile, a width of up to 18 miles, and a length of 277 miles, makes it one of the most significant natural landmarks in the United States. The park is divided into the North Rim and South Rim, each offering unique perspectives and experiences. The South Rim, open year-round, is the most accessible and popular section, featuring numerous viewpoints, historic sites, and visitor facilities. The North Rim, higher in elevation and less crowded, provides a more secluded experience and is open seasonally due to heavy snowfall in winter.

A journey to the Grand Canyon is an exploration of Earth's geological history. The layers of rock exposed in the canyon walls represent billions of years of history, with each stratum telling a story of the Earth's past. From the ancient Vishnu Basement Rocks at the bottom to the relatively younger Kaibab Limestone at the rim, the canyon is a natural museum of geology. This magnificent display is a paradise for geologists and nature enthusiasts alike, offering a profound perspective on the planet's evolutionary journey.

Beyond its geological significance, the Grand Canyon is also a place of profound cultural importance. The park is home to several Native American tribes, including the Havasupai, Hopi, Navajo, and Paiute. These communities have deep historical and spiritual connections to the canyon, reflected in their art, traditions, and cultural practices. The park strives to preserve and honor these indigenous cultures, providing visitors with an opportunity to learn about and respect these ancient connections.

The Grand Canyon National Park is not just about sightseeing; it's an adventurer's playground. It offers a plethora of outdoor activities, including hiking, rafting, mule rides, and camping. The Rim-to-Rim hike and the challenging descent to Phantom Ranch are popular among hiking enthusiasts.

16. Havasu Falls

Havasu Falls, a breathtaking oasis nestled in the heart of the Grand Canyon, is one of the most picturesque waterfalls in the world. Located within the Havasupai Indian Reservation in Arizona, this natural wonder is renowned for its stunning turquoise waters, cascading over a 100-foot drop into a series of inviting, travertine pools below. The falls are part of the Havasu Creek, which is fed by spring water and rich in calcium carbonate, giving the water its distinctive, mesmerizing color.

Reaching Havasu Falls is a rewarding challenge, involving a 10-mile hike from the trailhead at Hualapai Hilltop. The trail descends into the Havasu Canyon, passing through remote and rugged terrain, and offers a glimpse into the natural beauty and serenity of the area. Despite the arduous journey, the sight of the falls is instantly rejuvenating, making the trek worthwhile.

The area around Havasu Falls is a perfect spot for relaxation and exploration. Visitors can swim in the pools, lounge on the sandy shores, or explore nearby waterfalls, including Mooney Falls and Beaver Falls, each with its own unique beauty and ambiance. The area's lush vegetation and towering canyon walls provide a stark contrast to the otherwise arid landscape of the region.

Havasu Falls is not only a natural wonder but also a sacred site for the Havasupai Tribe, known as the "People of the Blue-Green Waters." The tribe has inhabited the Grand Canyon for centuries, and their culture and history are deeply intertwined with the land and water.

Due to its popularity and fragile ecosystem, access to Havasu Falls is limited, and permits are required. The Havasupai Tribe manages the area, and visitors must make reservations well in advance. The falls' remote location and the need for permits help preserve its pristine condition and the tranquility of the experience.

17. Vermilion Cliffs National Monument

Vermilion Cliffs National Monument, located in northern Arizona near the Utah border, is a breathtaking and remote landscape that captivates visitors with its stunning geological formations, vibrant colors, and sense of untouched wilderness. Established in 2000, this 280,000-acre monument is managed by the Bureau of Land Management and features dramatic cliffs, towering plateaus, deep canyons, and striking rock formations that have been sculpted over millions of years.

The most iconic features of Vermilion Cliffs National Monument include The Wave, Paria Canyon, and the Coyote Buttes. The Wave, located in the Coyote Buttes North area, is a world-famous sandstone rock formation known for its mesmerizing, wave-like patterns and vivid shades of red, orange, and gold. Because of its delicate nature and to preserve the area's beauty, access to The Wave is restricted to a limited number of permits per day, which are highly sought after by photographers and adventurers from around the globe.

Paria Canyon offers an extraordinary hiking experience through a labyrinth of narrow slot canyons and winding riverbeds, with towering sandstone walls that display a stunning array of colors and textures. The Paria River flows through the canyon, adding to the challenge and adventure of exploring this rugged and remote area. Hikers can also experience the breathtaking Buckskin Gulch, one of the longest and deepest slot canyons in the world.

In addition to its remarkable geological features, Vermilion Cliffs National Monument is home to diverse plant and animal life, including desert bighorn sheep, golden eagles, and the endangered California condor, which has been successfully reintroduced to the area. The monument's remote and rugged terrain provides a pristine habitat for wildlife and an unparalleled experience of solitude and natural beauty.

Visitors to Vermilion Cliffs National Monument can explore the area through guided tours, hiking, or off-road adventures. However, due to the remote and often challenging conditions, it is essential to come well-prepared and informed about the environment. The monument's raw and awe-inspiring landscapes offer an unforgettable experience for those seeking to witness the unspoiled beauty of the American Southwest.

18. Paria Canyon-Vermilion Cliffs Wilderness

The Paria Canyon-Vermilion Cliffs Wilderness, a spectacular and unspoiled region spanning 112,500 acres across northern Arizona and southern Utah, is a geological and ecological wonderland. Managed by the Bureau of Land Management, this wilderness area is famous for its towering cliffs, deep canyons, and diverse landscapes that range from arid desert to lush riparian zones.

One of the crown jewels of this wilderness is the Paria Canyon itself, offering one of the world's best slot canyon hiking experiences. The canyon features walls that rise hundreds of feet high but in some places are only a few feet apart. Hiking through Paria Canyon is an immersive experience, with the route following the meandering Paria River, crossing shallow water, and navigating around boulders and narrows.

The Vermilion Cliffs, the namesake of the wilderness, are a series of steep, eroded escarpments known for their vibrant, swirling colors and striking formations. The most famous section of the cliffs is the Wave, a mesmerizing rock formation known for its undulating, wave-like structure and the interplay of red, orange, and yellow sandstone.

Buckskin Gulch, a tributary of the Paria River, is claimed to be the longest and deepest slot canyon in the Southwest. Hiking through Buckskin Gulch is a unique adventure, requiring preparation and respect for the challenging conditions often found in slot canyons.

The wilderness area is also a haven for wildlife and a hotspot for biodiversity. It's home to various species adapted to the desert environment, including coyotes, bobcats, mountain lions, and a variety of bird species. The riparian areas along the Paria River support a lush array of vegetation, providing a stark contrast to the surrounding desert.

19. Horseshoe Bend

Horseshoe Bend, a remarkable natural phenomenon located near the town of Page in Northern Arizona, is one of the most iconic and photographed natural landmarks in the United States. This dramatic meander in the Colorado River creates a near-perfect circular bend, forming a horseshoe-like shape that has captivated the imaginations of photographers, nature lovers, and travelers from around the globe.

Situated just downstream from the Glen Canyon Dam and Lake Powell, Horseshoe Bend is easily accessible and presents an awe-inspiring sight. The viewpoint is reached via a 1.5-mile round-trip hike over a sandy trail, which leads to the edge of a steep cliff that drops 1,000 feet straight down to the river below. The sight of the emerald-green river making a 270-degree turn around a red sandstone escarpment is nothing short of breathtaking.

The geology of Horseshoe Bend is as fascinating as its beauty. Over millions of years, the Colorado River has eroded the landscape, cutting through layers of sandstone and limestone to carve the bend. This natural process has created not just a visual spectacle but also a testament to the power and persistence of natural forces. The layers of rock visible in the canyon walls tell a story of the Earth's geological history, making Horseshoe Bend a point of interest for geologists and nature enthusiasts alike.

Photography at Horseshoe Bend is particularly popular, with the viewpoint offering panoramic views that are perfect for capturing the grandeur of the landscape. The best times for photography are sunrise and sunset when the lighting adds a dramatic effect to the already stunning scenery. The interplay of light and shadow, along with the changing colors of the sky, enhance the natural beauty of the bend.

Horseshoe Bend is more than just a picturesque spot; it's a destination that inspires awe and reflection. It represents the beauty and power of the natural world and provides a space for visitors to connect with the environment. Whether standing at the edge of the cliff, capturing the perfect photograph, or simply soaking in the view, Horseshoe Bend offers a truly unforgettable experience.

In conclusion, Horseshoe Bend is a must-visit landmark for anyone traveling in Northern Arizona. Its easy accessibility, combined with its stunning natural beauty, makes it a highlight for visitors to the region.

20. Lake Powell

Lake Powell, a stunning reservoir on the Colorado River, is one of the most popular recreational destinations in the American Southwest. Stretching across the border between Utah and Arizona, this massive, man-made lake was created by the construction of the Glen Canyon Dam in the 1960s. Spanning over 186 miles in length, Lake Powell boasts more than 2,000 miles of scenic shoreline, dotted with towering red rock cliffs, hidden coves, sandy beaches, and striking geological formations.

The lake's turquoise waters set against the backdrop of the surrounding red and orange sandstone cliffs create a breathtaking contrast that attracts millions of visitors each year. The beauty and diversity of the landscape make Lake Powell a haven for outdoor enthusiasts, offering a wide range of recreational activities. Boating is one of the most popular ways to explore the lake, and visitors can rent houseboats, speedboats, or kayaks to navigate the winding waterways and discover hidden canyons and secluded spots.

Fishing is another favorite pastime, with the lake teeming with a variety of fish species, including striped bass, walleye, and largemouth bass. The warm waters are perfect for swimming, water skiing, paddleboarding, and other water sports, making Lake Powell an ideal destination for families and thrill-seekers alike.

One of the most awe-inspiring natural wonders in the area is Rainbow Bridge National Monument, one of the world's largest natural stone arches. Accessible by boat and a short hike, this incredible rock formation is a sacred site for Native American tribes and a must-see landmark for visitors.

Camping along Lake Powell's shoreline or staying at one of the many marinas and resorts offers an unforgettable experience under the starry desert sky. The Glen Canyon National Recreation Area, which encompasses Lake Powell, provides numerous hiking trails, breathtaking overlooks, and opportunities to learn about the area's rich history and geology.

Whether you're seeking adventure on the water, relaxation in a serene desert setting, or a chance to marvel at nature's wonders, Lake Powell is a captivating destination that promises an unforgettable experience for all who visit.

21. Antelope Canyon

Antelope Canyon, a mesmerizing natural wonder located in the heart of the Navajo Nation in Northern Arizona, stands as one of the most exquisite examples of slot canyon formations in the world. This awe-inspiring geological marvel, sculpted by the relentless force of water and wind over millions of years, captivates visitors with its undulating walls, narrow passageways, and the interplay of light and shadow.

Comprising two separate sections, the Upper Antelope Canyon (Tsé bighánílíní - 'the place where water runs through rocks') and the Lower Antelope Canyon (Hazdistazí - 'spiral rock arches'), each part of the canyon offers a unique experience. The Upper Canyon, known for its accessibility and light beams that shine down into the openings of the canyon, creates an almost ethereal atmosphere. The light beams are most prominent during the midday sun, illuminating the canyon's orange-pink sandstone walls in a breathtaking display.

In contrast, the Lower Canyon is a more narrow and winding section, known for its "spiral" rock formations and the adventurous descent required to enter the canyon. This part of the canyon, while less visited, offers an equally stunning visual experience, with its intricate rock formations and play of colors.

Photographers and nature enthusiasts from around the world flock to Antelope Canyon to capture its unique beauty. The array of colors and shapes makes it a photographer's paradise, especially when the sun's rays peek into the canyon, creating a mesmerizing dance of light and shadow.

Antelope Canyon was formed by the erosion of Navajo Sandstone, primarily due to flash flooding. Rainwater, particularly during monsoon season, runs into the extensive basin above the slot canyon sections, picking up speed and sand as it rushes into the narrow passageways. Over time, this process has deepened and smoothed the corridors into flowing shapes that visitors see today.

Visiting Antelope Canyon is only possible through guided tours, in adherence to Navajo Nation regulations. These tours are led by experienced guides, who share insights about the canyon's geology, history, and cultural significance to the Navajo people. This protective measure ensures the preservation of the site and offers a respectful way to experience this sacred place.

22. Monument Valley

Monument Valley, a sprawling and majestic area straddling the Arizona-Utah border, is a geological masterpiece that epitomizes the wild and rugged beauty of the American Southwest. Renowned for its towering sandstone buttes, the valley is not just a natural wonder but a cultural icon, deeply ingrained in the American psyche through countless films, photographs, and artworks.

Covering a vast area of the Colorado Plateau, Monument Valley is part of the Navajo Nation Reservation. The Valley's unique landscape has been shaped over millions of years by the forces of erosion, carving out these dramatic formations that rise majestically from the desert floor. The tallest of these, the West and East Mitten Buttes, resemble hands reaching towards the sky and have become symbols of the American West.

The Navajo people, who call this land home, refer to Monument Valley as Tsé Bii' Ndzisgaii, meaning "the valley of the rocks." For them, it's not just a scenic backdrop but a sacred space imbued with spiritual significance and a rich tapestry of cultural history. Guided tours, often led by Navajo guides, offer visitors insights into the valley's geology, flora, fauna, and the Navajo traditions and stories connected to the land.

Monument Valley's otherworldly landscape has captivated filmmakers and artists for decades, making it a quintessential location for Western films. Its stark, awe-inspiring scenery has provided the backdrop for numerous movies, from John Ford's classic Westerns to modern blockbusters, embedding it firmly in global popular culture.

For visitors, the experience of Monument Valley extends beyond sightseeing. Driving along the Valley Drive, a 17-mile dirt road that winds through the most iconic formations, is an immersive journey through a landscape that feels timeless. Each turn offers a new perspective of the valley's towering spires and vast, open skies, presenting an unparalleled opportunity for photography.

Sunrise and sunset are particularly magical times in Monument Valley. The play of light and shadow transforms the landscape, with the buttes and mesas glowing in hues of orange, red, and purple. These moments of natural spectacle underscore the serene and majestic presence of the valley.

23. Navajo National Monument

Navajo National Monument, located in the northwest corner of the Navajo Nation in Arizona, is a testament to the ancient history and enduring legacy of the Ancestral Puebloan people. Established in 1909, this monument preserves three of the most well-preserved cliff dwellings of the Ancestral Puebloans: Keet Seel (Kits'iil), Betatakin (Bitát'ahkin), and Inscription House (Ts'ah Bii' Kin). These sites are extraordinary examples of the architectural skills of the ancient Puebloans, nestled in secluded canyons and offering a glimpse into their daily lives over 700 years ago.

The monument's most accessible site, Betatakin, can be viewed from an overlook near the visitor center or on a guided hike. Keet Seel, the largest and best-preserved ruin, requires a more strenuous effort to visit, involving a lengthy hike, but offers an unparalleled experience of exploring an ancient village that appears much as it did centuries ago. Inscription House, currently closed to the public, is another remarkable site that showcases the engineering prowess of its ancient builders.

Navajo National Monument is more than an archaeological site; it is a place of profound cultural and spiritual significance for the Navajo people. The monument offers visitors the opportunity to learn about Navajo culture, history, and traditions, providing a deeper understanding of the people who have lived in this region for centuries.

The surrounding landscape of the monument is a rugged terrain of canyons, mesas, and high desert, offering spectacular views and a chance to experience the solitude and beauty of the Colorado Plateau. The area is home to a variety of wildlife, and the vegetation ranges from desert scrub to Ponderosa Pine forests, providing a diverse ecological experience.

Navajo National Monument, situated in Northern Arizona on the Navajo Nation Reservation, is a historic and cultural treasure preserving some of the best-preserved cliff dwellings of the Ancestral Puebloan people. This national monument is a testament to the ancient history and enduring legacy of these indigenous communities.

24. Canyon de Chelly National Monument

Canyon de Chelly National Monument, located in northeastern Arizona near Chinle, is a breathtaking natural wonder and a place of deep historical and cultural significance. Spanning approximately 84,000 acres, the monument is part of the Navajo Nation and is co-managed by the National Park Service and Navajo tribal authorities, making it unique among U.S. national monuments.

The canyon is renowned for its striking red sandstone cliffs, which rise up to 1,000 feet (300 meters) above the canyon floor, creating a stunning contrast against the arid desert landscape. Over millions of years, the forces of water and wind sculpted this intricate labyrinth of gorges and mesas. The monument encompasses two main canyons, Canyon de Chelly and Canyon del Muerto, both of which offer spectacular views and numerous points of interest.

Canyon de Chelly has been continuously inhabited for nearly 5,000 years, making it one of North America's oldest continuously occupied sites. Ancient Puebloans, also known as Ancestral Puebloans, were among its earliest inhabitants, leaving behind intricate cliff dwellings and petroglyphs that tell stories of their lives and beliefs. Later, Hopi and Navajo people made the canyon their home, and it remains a sacred site for the Navajo Nation today.

Visitors to the monument can explore the canyon through guided tours led by Navajo guides, who share insights into the area's history, geology, and cultural significance. Highlights include the White House Ruin, one of the most famous cliff dwellings, and Spider Rock, a towering 800-foot (240-meter) spire that holds special importance in Navajo folklore as the home of Spider Woman, a key figure in their mythology.

The canyon offers hiking, horseback riding, and photography opportunities, along with scenic drives along its rim. Each experience provides a deeper connection to the canyon's rich heritage and stunning natural beauty. Canyon de Chelly National Monument is more than a geological marvel; it is a living testament to the resilience and spirituality of the people who have called it home for millennia.

25. Petrified Forest National Park

Petrified Forest National Park, located in Northeastern Arizona, is a surreal landscape that takes visitors back in time. Spanning over 220,000 acres, this unique park is famous for its vast deposits of brilliantly colored petrified wood, remnants of a prehistoric forest transformed into quartz over millions of years.

The park's landscape is a mosaic of colors, from the deep reds and oranges of the petrified wood to the multi-hued badlands of the Painted Desert. The park's northern region, the Painted Desert, is particularly striking, with its hills and buttes showcasing a vibrant spectrum of colors.

Petrified Forest is not just about petrified wood; it's also rich in fossils, providing insights into the Late Triassic period. The park's paleontological resources include fossils of early dinosaurs, reptiles, and plants, making it a significant site for scientific research.

The park's human history is equally fascinating, with numerous archaeological sites and petroglyphs providing evidence of early human occupation. Puerco Pueblo and Newspaper Rock are two such sites where visitors can see ancient petroglyphs up close.

Trails and overlooks throughout Petrified Forest National Park offer various ways to experience its unique landscape, whether it's a leisurely walk along the Crystal Forest Trail, a hike through the Blue Mesa badlands, or a scenic drive along the park's 28-mile road. Each trail and overlook provides a different perspective of this unique landscape, from the shimmering pieces of petrified wood to the sweeping vistas of the Painted Desert.

In conclusion, each of these destinations in Arizona - Wupatki National Monument, Jerome, Lake Powell, and Petrified Forest National Park - offers a unique and enriching experience. From ancient ruins and historic towns to stunning natural landscapes and geological wonders, these sites represent the diverse and rich tapestry of Arizona's cultural and natural heritage.

Southern Arizona

1. Ajo

Nestled in the heart of the Sonoran Desert in southwestern Arizona, Ajo is a hidden gem that offers visitors a unique blend of natural beauty, rich history, and a vibrant arts community. This charming town, originally a mining town, has evolved into a welcoming destination for those seeking a peaceful retreat amidst the desert's rugged landscape.

Ajo's history is closely tied to its copper mining heritage, and the remnants of this industry are still visible today. The New Cornelia Open Pit Mine, one of the largest copper mines in the United States, offers a glimpse into the town's mining past. Visitors can take guided tours to witness the massive scale of the pit and learn about the mining processes that shaped the town's history.

One of the town's standout features is the Ajo Plaza, a picturesque central square surrounded by Spanish colonial-style buildings. The plaza serves as a focal point for the community and hosts various events and gatherings throughout the year. Strolling through Ajo Plaza, you'll encounter local shops, restaurants, and art galleries that showcase the talents of the town's creative residents.

Nature enthusiasts will find Ajo to be an ideal base for exploring the nearby Cabeza Prieta National Wildlife Refuge, known for its unique desert ecosystems and wildlife. The refuge offers opportunities for hiking, birdwatching, and wildlife photography. Ajo's location also makes it a gateway to the Organ Pipe Cactus National Monument, famous for its impressive cactus forests and scenic drives.

Art lovers will be delighted by the town's vibrant arts scene. Ajo is home to the Ajo Council for the Fine Arts, which hosts exhibitions, workshops, and cultural events that celebrate the creative spirit of the community. The town's artists often draw inspiration from the stunning desert landscapes that surround them, creating works that reflect the beauty and mystique of the Sonoran Desert.

2. Organ Pipe Cactus National Monument

Organ Pipe Cactus National Monument, located in southern Arizona along the border with Mexico, is a breathtakingly beautiful and ecologically rich desert landscape that celebrates the diverse flora and fauna of the Sonoran Desert. Designated as a UNESCO Biosphere Reserve, this 517-square-mile monument is named for the organ pipe cactus, a unique species that thrives in this region and can be found in abundance throughout the park. The monument is the only place in the United States where this particular cactus grows naturally, making it a must-visit destination for nature enthusiasts and plant lovers.

The dramatic desert landscape of Organ Pipe Cactus National Monument is defined by towering saguaro cacti, rugged mountain ranges, and sweeping valleys covered with a stunning variety of desert vegetation. Visitors can experience the striking beauty of this remote wilderness through an array of activities, including hiking, scenic drives, and wildlife observation. The park's many trails, ranging from short nature walks to challenging backcountry hikes, offer opportunities to explore the desert's unique ecosystems and enjoy panoramic views of the surrounding mountains and valleys.

One of the most popular ways to explore the monument is by taking the Ajo Mountain Drive, a 21-mile scenic loop that winds through some of the park's most spectacular landscapes. Along the way, visitors can marvel at the abundance of organ pipe cacti and other native plants while stopping at designated viewpoints to take in the breathtaking desert scenery. The drive also provides access to several trailheads, where hikers can further immerse themselves in the natural beauty of the area.

Wildlife enthusiasts will be delighted by the diverse array of animals that call the monument home, including desert bighorn sheep, coyotes, javelinas, and a variety of bird species. The desert is especially vibrant in the spring, when wildflowers bloom in brilliant colors, adding to the allure of the landscape.

Organ Pipe Cactus National Monument offers a serene and awe-inspiring escape into one of North America's most diverse and beautiful deserts. Whether you're hiking through its rugged terrain or simply enjoying the tranquility of the desert, the monument provides a memorable experience for anyone who appreciates the wonders of the natural world.

3. Tohono O'odham Nation Cultural Center and Museum

The Tohono O'odham Nation Cultural Center and Museum, situated in Sells, offers a profound journey into the history, traditions, and contemporary life of the Tohono O'odham people. As one of the indigenous tribes of the American Southwest, the Tohono O'odham have a rich cultural heritage that spans centuries, and this museum provides a window into their world.

The museum houses a remarkable collection of artifacts, artwork, and exhibits that tell the story of the Tohono O'odham people. Visitors can explore the tribe's history, from their traditional ways of life to their encounters with European explorers, missionaries, and settlers. The exhibits highlight the resilience and adaptability of the Tohono O'odham, who have maintained their cultural identity while embracing change.

One of the museum's central themes is the Tohono O'odham language. Visitors can learn about the unique language, its importance in preserving cultural traditions, and efforts to revitalize and teach it to younger generations. The Tohono O'odham people have a rich oral tradition, and the language plays a vital role in passing down stories, songs, and cultural knowledge.

The museum also showcases a wide range of traditional crafts and artwork created by Tohono O'odham artisans. From intricately woven baskets to colorful pottery and vibrant beadwork, these pieces reflect the tribe's artistic talents and cultural expressions. Visitors can appreciate the craftsmanship and creativity that go into each work of art.

Throughout the year, the Tohono O'odham Nation Cultural Center and Museum hosts cultural events, workshops, and demonstrations that allow visitors to engage with the living culture of the Tohono O'odham people. Traditional dance performances, storytelling sessions, and hands-on activities provide an interactive and immersive experience, deepening one's appreciation for the tribe's customs and traditions.

The museum is not only a place of learning but also a vital resource for the Tohono O'odham community itself. It serves as a hub for cultural preservation, education, and community engagement. The Tohono O'odham Nation places great importance on sharing its heritage with both tribal members and the wider public, fostering a greater understanding of the tribe's contributions to the cultural tapestry of the American Southwest.

4. Kitt Peak National Observatory

Perched atop the rugged mountains of the Sonoran Desert in southern Arizona, Kitt Peak National Observatory is an astronomical wonderland that beckons stargazers, scientists, and curious visitors from around the world. This premier astronomical research facility is home to some of the most advanced telescopes on Earth, offering a captivating journey into the cosmos and the frontiers of space exploration.

Kitt Peak's history as an astronomical site dates back to the mid-20th century when the National Science Foundation established the observatory. Today, it hosts 24 optical and radio telescopes, each dedicated to exploring different aspects of the universe. The most iconic of these telescopes is the Mayall 4-meter telescope, which has been instrumental in numerous groundbreaking discoveries, such as mapping the structure of the universe and studying the motion of galaxies.

Visitors to Kitt Peak National Observatory are treated to guided tours that provide insights into the science behind these telescopes and the mysteries of the cosmos they seek to unravel. The observatory offers daytime and evening programs, allowing guests to observe the sun, stars, planets, and distant galaxies through powerful telescopes. On a clear night, the night sky at Kitt Peak is a mesmerizing tableau of stars, planets, and celestial wonders that will leave you in awe of the universe's vastness.

Kitt Peak also serves as an educational hub, welcoming students, researchers, and astronomers from all over the world. The observatory conducts public outreach programs and hosts workshops and lectures that provide a deeper understanding of our place in the cosmos. It's a place where the wonders of science and the beauty of the night sky come together to inspire and educate.

The location of Kitt Peak Observatory, away from urban light pollution, ensures pristine conditions for stargazing. The observatory's elevation of 6,875 feet above sea level and the dry desert air contribute to exceptionally clear and dark skies, making it an ideal destination for amateur astronomers and astrophotographers.

5. Tubac

Nestled in the picturesque Santa Cruz River Valley in southern Arizona, Tubac is a charming and historic town known for its artistic ambiance, Spanish colonial heritage, and vibrant cultural scene. Founded in 1752 as a Spanish presidio, Tubac is one of the oldest European settlements in Arizona, and its rich history is beautifully preserved.

Tubac's historic district is a treasure trove of adobe buildings, cobbled streets, and art galleries that showcase the talents of local and regional artists. The town has a thriving arts community, and it's not uncommon to encounter painters, sculptors, and craftsmen at work in their studios. The Tubac Center of the Arts hosts exhibitions, workshops, and events that celebrate the creative spirit of the town.

One of Tubac's standout attractions is the Tubac Presidio State Historic Park, which preserves the site of the original Spanish presidio. Visitors can explore the museum, historic buildings, and gardens, gaining insights into the area's colonial past and the challenges faced by early settlers.

Tubac also offers opportunities for outdoor recreation, with nearby hiking and birdwatching trails that allow visitors to experience the stunning desert landscapes and the lush riparian habitat along the Santa Cruz River. The Tumacácori National Historical Park, just a short drive away, offers a chance to explore mission ruins and learn about the region's Spanish colonial history.

Food enthusiasts will appreciate Tubac's dining scene, which features a mix of southwestern and Mexican cuisine, as well as international flavors. The town's charming eateries and restaurants serve up delectable dishes in a relaxed, small-town atmosphere.

Throughout the year, Tubac hosts cultural festivals, art fairs, and events that draw visitors and artists from all over the region. The Tubac Festival of the Arts, held each February, is one of the town's most renowned events, featuring a diverse range of art, music, and culinary delights.

In conclusion, Tubac is a captivating destination that seamlessly blends history, art, and natural beauty. Whether you're exploring the historic streets, discovering local artwork, or immersing yourself in the desert landscapes, Tubac offers a delightful and enriching experience that reflects the unique cultural tapestry of southern Arizona.

6. Tumacácori National Historical Park

Tumacácori National Historical Park, located in the upper Santa Cruz River Valley of southern Arizona, preserves the ruins of three Spanish colonial missions. Founded in the late 17th century by Jesuit and later Franciscan missionaries, the park provides a window into the region's early history, including the interactions between European settlers and the Native American communities.

The main attraction of the park is the Tumacácori Mission, established by Jesuit padre Eusebio Kino in 1691. The mission's partially restored church and convento offer visitors a glimpse into the Spanish colonial era. The park also includes the ruins of the Guevavi and Calabazas missions, accessible only through ranger-led tours.

Visitors to Tumacácori can explore the mission grounds, visit the museum, and participate in various educational programs. The museum houses artifacts and exhibits that tell the story of the missions and the people who lived there, including the O'odham, Yaqui, and Apache.

The park also features a section of the Juan Bautista de Anza National Historic Trail. This trail commemorates the route taken by Anza in 1775-76 during his expedition to establish a settlement at San Francisco Bay. Along the trail, visitors can enjoy the scenic beauty of the Santa Cruz River Valley and learn about the region's diverse ecosystems.

Tumacácori National Historical Park is a place of historical reflection and natural beauty, offering insights into Arizona's early history and the enduring legacy of its diverse cultures.

7. Patagonia Lake State Park

Patagonia Lake State Park, located in the rolling hills of southeastern Arizona, offers a serene and picturesque escape into the heart of the Sonoran Desert. The park centers around a 265-acre man-made lake, created by the damming of Sonoita Creek, providing a tranquil setting for a wide range of recreational activities and a diverse array of flora and fauna.

The centerpiece of Patagonia Lake State Park is the crystal-clear lake itself, surrounded by a beautiful desert landscape and a backdrop of the Patagonia Mountains. The lake is a haven for water enthusiasts, offering opportunities for fishing, boating, and kayaking. Anglers can cast their lines in search of a variety of fish species, including bass, catfish, and trout. The park provides boat rentals and a marina for those who want to explore the lake by water.

For birdwatchers, Patagonia Lake is a paradise, with over 300 bird species documented in the area. The park's diverse habitats, including marshes, grasslands, and riparian areas, attract migratory and resident birds throughout the year. It's a prime location for spotting waterfowl, songbirds, and raptors, making it a popular destination for birdwatching enthusiasts.

Patagonia Lake State Park boasts a network of well-maintained hiking and nature trails that wind through the desert landscape, allowing visitors to immerse themselves in the region's natural beauty. The trails offer opportunities for wildlife viewing, as well as a chance to encounter desert plants and cacti in their native habitat. The park also provides picnic areas, shaded ramadas, and a sandy beach, making it an ideal spot for picnics, family gatherings, and relaxation.

The park offers both day-use and camping facilities, with campgrounds equipped with modern amenities, including restrooms, showers, and RV hookups. Camping at Patagonia Lake State Park allows you to experience the tranquil desert nights, with opportunities for stargazing in the clear, unpolluted skies.

Throughout the year, the park hosts various educational programs and events, such as guided nature walks, birding tours, and evening campfire programs. These activities provide visitors with a deeper understanding of the natural and cultural history of the region.

8. Ramsey Canyon Preserve

Nestled in the Huachuca Mountains of southeastern Arizona, Ramsey Canyon Preserve is a pristine oasis of biodiversity and natural beauty that beckons nature enthusiasts, birdwatchers, and hikers alike. This sanctuary, managed by the Nature Conservancy, boasts a lush and verdant canyon, a contrast to the surrounding arid landscapes of the region.

What sets Ramsey Canyon apart is its unique microclimate. The canyon's elevation and proximity to underground springs create a cool, moist environment that supports a diverse range of plant and animal species. Towering sycamore and oak trees provide shade and habitat for a variety of wildlife, while the year-round flow of Ramsey Creek sustains this verdant paradise.

Birdwatchers flock to Ramsey Canyon for the opportunity to spot numerous avian species, including the elegant and elusive Elegant Trogon. The preserve is part of the Upper San Pedro River Basin, designated as an Important Bird Area, and offers prime birdwatching opportunities throughout the year. The lush vegetation and abundant insects attract a wide range of bird species, making it a hotspot for ornithological enthusiasts.

Visitors can explore Ramsey Canyon via well-maintained trails that wind through the preserve, offering a chance to observe the diverse flora and fauna up close. The most popular trail is the Ramsey Canyon Trail, which leads to a charming pond surrounded by hummingbird feeders, providing a unique opportunity to witness these tiny, colorful birds in action.

The preserve also offers educational programs, guided nature walks, and birdwatching tours led by knowledgeable naturalists. These programs provide visitors with insights into the canyon's ecology, geology, and the importance of conservation efforts to protect this unique habitat.

Ramsey Canyon Preserve serves not only as a sanctuary for wildlife but also as a living laboratory for scientific research and a testament to the importance of preserving fragile ecosystems in the face of environmental challenges. It is a place of serenity and natural wonder, where visitors can connect with the beauty and complexity of the natural world.

9. Bisbee

Bisbee, nestled in the Mule Mountains of southeastern Arizona, is a charming and historic mining town that has transformed into a vibrant arts and cultural destination. Once the largest city between St. Louis and San Francisco, Bisbee is now renowned for its well-preserved Victorian architecture, quirky artistic community, and unique history.

The town's mining history is evident in its landscape and architecture. The Copper Queen Mine, one of the oldest and most productive copper mines in Arizona, offers underground mine tours that transport visitors back in time to experience a miner's life. The Bisbee Mining & Historical Museum, part of the Smithsonian Institution's Affiliate Museum program, provides further insights into the town's rich mining heritage.

Bisbee's artistic flair is evident in its numerous galleries, studios, and boutiques. The town's creative atmosphere is fostered by a thriving community of artists, musicians, and writers. The winding, hilly streets of Bisbee are filled with colorful, historic buildings housing unique shops, galleries, and eateries, making it an ideal destination for leisurely exploration and shopping.

The town also hosts various events and festivals throughout the year, celebrating its eclectic culture and community spirit. Events like the Bisbee 1000 Great Stair Climb and the Bisbee Pride Weekend attract visitors from all over, adding to the town's lively and inclusive atmosphere.

Bisbee's location in the scenic mountains of Arizona offers outdoor enthusiasts a range of activities, including hiking, bird watching, and exploring the surrounding landscapes. The town's moderate climate and scenic beauty make it a perfect getaway for those seeking a blend of history, culture, and outdoor adventure.

10. Tombstone

Tombstone, famously known as "The Town Too Tough To Die," is steeped in Wild West history. Established in 1879, this historic town was the site of the infamous Gunfight at the O.K. Corral, which epitomized the lawlessness and adventure of the American frontier. Today, Tombstone offers a well-preserved glimpse into the late 19th-century mining town life and remains a symbol of the rugged spirit of the Old West.

Situated in Southeast Arizona, Tombstone was one of the last boomtowns. Silver mining brought prosperity and attracted a mix of entrepreneurs, miners, outlaws, and gunslingers. The resulting blend of wealth and lawlessness set the stage for the town's storied past, which included not only mining successes but also notorious events like the gunfight involving Wyatt Earp, Doc Holliday, and the Clanton-McLaury gang.

Visitors to Tombstone can walk on the same wooden boardwalks along Allen Street where historic figures once strolled. The town is filled with attractions that transport you back to the 1880s, including saloons, museums, and the Bird Cage Theatre, known as one of the wildest places in the West. Daily reenactments of the O.K. Corral gunfight are a must-see, offering a dramatic portrayal of Tombstone's most famous event.

The Tombstone Courthouse State Historic Park, an impressive Victorian structure, now serves as a museum chronicling the town's history. Exhibits showcase artifacts from Tombstone's mining and ranching days, offering insight into the lives of the town's early inhabitants.

Beyond its historical attractions, Tombstone celebrates its heritage with various events throughout the year, such as Helldorado Days and Wyatt Earp Days, featuring parades, gunfight reenactments, and street entertainment.

11. Chiricahua National Monument

Chiricahua National Monument, located in southeastern Arizona, is a hidden gem of the National Park System. Spanning approximately 12,000 acres, this monument is often referred to as the "Wonderland of Rocks," a fitting description for its stunning array of rock spires, balancing rocks, and natural bridges formed from volcanic activity millions of years ago.

The monument's landscape is a result of a massive volcanic eruption that spewed ash over 1,200 square miles. Erosion over millions of years sculpted this ash into the breathtaking rock formations seen today. The pinnacles, spires, and balanced rocks create an almost otherworldly scene, drawing visitors from around the world.

Chiricahua offers over 17 miles of day-use hiking trails, ranging from easy walks to challenging hikes, which lead visitors through its diverse ecosystems. The Echo Canyon Loop and the Heart of Rocks Loop are particularly popular, offering close-up views of the monument's most famous rock formations. Along these trails, visitors can also encounter a variety of plant and animal life, including species unique to the Chiricahua Mountains.

The monument is not only a geological wonder but also a place of rich biodiversity. It is a designated Important Bird Area, with over 200 bird species recorded, making it a paradise for birdwatchers. The diverse habitats, from high desert to mountain woodlands, support a variety of wildlife, including deer, javelinas, and coatimundis.

In addition to its natural beauty, Chiricahua has a fascinating human history. The area was once home to the Chiricahua Apache, and later became a hideout for outlaws. The historic Faraway Ranch, located within the monument, offers a glimpse into the pioneer life and the early days of tourism in the area.

12. Cochise Stronghold

Nestled within the rugged Dragoon Mountains of southeastern Arizona, Cochise Stronghold is a place of natural beauty and historical significance that beckons adventurers and history enthusiasts alike. This remote and picturesque canyon was named after the renowned Apache chief Cochise, who used it as a refuge during the Apache Wars in the late 19th century.

Cochise Stronghold's dramatic landscape consists of towering rock formations, deep canyons, and lush vegetation, creating a sanctuary for wildlife and a haven for hikers, rock climbers, and outdoor enthusiasts. The area offers numerous hiking trails that wind through the rugged terrain, providing stunning vistas and opportunities to explore the unique flora and fauna of the Chiricahua Mountains.

One of the most popular trails is the Cochise Stronghold Trail, which takes hikers on a journey through the heart of the canyon. As you hike, you'll encounter evidence of the Apache people who once called this place home, including ancient petroglyphs etched into the rocks. The trail leads to the Stronghold Dome, a prominent rock formation that attracts rock climbers from around the world due to its challenging routes and breathtaking views.

For history enthusiasts, Cochise Stronghold offers the opportunity to delve into the turbulent past of the American Southwest. Cochise and his band of Chiricahua Apaches used the area's natural defenses to resist U.S. Army forces during the Apache Wars. Visitors can explore the area's historical markers and imagine the challenges faced by both the Apache people and the settlers during this period.

Camping is available in the nearby Dragoon Mountains, providing a unique opportunity to experience the serenity of the desert night sky and the soothing sounds of nature. Cochise Stronghold is also within a reasonable drive of the Chiricahua National Monument, another natural wonderland known for its towering rock pinnacles and hiking trails.

In conclusion, Cochise Stronghold is a rugged and picturesque destination that combines outdoor adventure with a rich historical backdrop. It's a place where the spirit of Cochise and the Apache people lives on, and where visitors can immerse themselves in the beauty and history of the American Southwest.

13. Kartchner Caverns State Park

Kartchner Caverns State Park, located near Benson, Arizona, is a mesmerizing natural wonder that offers visitors a chance to explore one of the most pristine and beautifully preserved cave systems in the United States. Discovered in 1974 by two cavers, Randy Tufts and Gary Tenen, and kept secret for many years to ensure its protection, the caverns were eventually developed into a state park that opened to the public in 1999. Today, Kartchner Caverns is celebrated for its stunning formations, intricate limestone passages, and commitment to conservation.

The cave system, formed over hundreds of thousands of years, features a breathtaking array of speleothems, or cave formations, including massive stalactites, stalagmites, soda straws, and delicate helictites. One of the most impressive formations is the 58-foot-tall "Kubla Khan" column, the tallest of its kind in Arizona. The caverns are also home to delicate drapery formations, flowstones, and a host of other geological wonders, all of which create an awe-inspiring underground landscape.

Visitors can choose from guided tours that showcase the caverns' incredible beauty while highlighting the park's emphasis on preservation. The Rotunda/Throne Room Tour takes visitors through chambers adorned with spectacular formations, while the Big Room Tour, available seasonally, allows guests to experience an area that serves as a crucial roosting site for bats. Throughout each tour, knowledgeable guides share fascinating insights into the cave's history, geology, and the measures taken to preserve its pristine condition.

The state park also features a Discovery Center, which offers interactive exhibits, educational displays, and a chance to learn more about the cave's ecosystem, formation, and the story of its discovery. Above ground, visitors can enjoy hiking trails that wind through the desert landscape, providing opportunities to see native wildlife and panoramic views of the surrounding area.

Kartchner Caverns State Park offers a rare opportunity to experience the wonders of an extraordinary cave system while emphasizing the importance of conservation and responsible exploration. A visit to these caverns is a truly unforgettable experience, showcasing the hidden beauty and geological marvels that lie beneath the Arizona desert.

14. Elgin and Sonoita

Elgin and Sonoita, two charming towns in southeastern Arizona, offer a delightful blend of rolling vineyards, open landscapes, and a laid-back, rural atmosphere. Nestled in the heart of Arizona's wine country, this region is a hidden gem for wine enthusiasts, nature lovers, and those seeking a peaceful escape from the hustle and bustle of city life.

Elgin and Sonoita are at the center of Arizona's burgeoning wine industry, with vineyards and wineries dotting the landscape. The high-altitude terrain and cool climate create ideal conditions for growing grapes, resulting in award-winning wines that have gained recognition both locally and nationally. Visitors can explore the numerous wineries, tasting rooms, and vineyard tours that showcase the diverse varietals produced in the area.

Among the acclaimed wineries in the region is the Sonoita Vineyards, one of Arizona's oldest and most respected wineries. Their picturesque tasting room offers visitors the chance to sample a variety of wines while enjoying panoramic views of the surrounding countryside.

Beyond wine, Elgin and Sonoita are surrounded by pristine wilderness and rolling grasslands, making it an excellent destination for outdoor activities. Birdwatchers flock to the region, as it's home to a diverse array of bird species, including the elegant Montezuma quail and a variety of raptors.

Hiking and horseback riding opportunities abound, with numerous trails meandering through the rolling hills and offering breathtaking vistas of the Santa Rita Mountains. The region is also renowned for its dark skies, making it an excellent spot for stargazing and astrophotography.

The towns of Elgin and Sonoita offer a range of accommodation options, from cozy bed and breakfasts to guest ranches and vacation rentals. The local restaurants and eateries showcase farm-to-table cuisine, often featuring locally sourced ingredients and regional flavors.

Throughout the year, the region hosts a variety of events and festivals that celebrate its agricultural heritage and vibrant arts scene. The annual Sonoita Horse Races, held every Labor Day weekend, draw visitors from far and wide for a day of equestrian excitement.

15. Madera Canyon

Nestled in the heart of the Santa Rita Mountains in southern Arizona, Madera Canyon stands as a testament to the breathtaking beauty and biodiversity of the American Southwest. Spanning an elevation range from 4,000 to 9,000 feet, Madera Canyon is a natural gem that beckons nature enthusiasts, hikers, birdwatchers, and outdoor adventurers from around the world.

One of the most captivating aspects of Madera Canyon is its diverse ecosystem. The canyon boasts a unique blend of desert, mountain, and riparian environments, creating a haven for a rich array of plant and animal species. As you traverse the canyon's network of trails, you'll encounter towering Sycamore and Douglas fir trees, alongside desert vegetation like saguaros and prickly pear cacti. This extraordinary mix of flora makes Madera Canyon a year-round destination, with each season offering its own charm.

Perhaps the most renowned attraction in Madera Canyon is its vibrant birdlife. Birdwatchers flock to the region to catch glimpses of over 250 bird species, including the elegant hummingbirds that frequent the canyon. The aptly named Santa Rita Lodge serves as a hub for bird enthusiasts, offering numerous feeding stations and expert guides who help visitors spot a variety of feathered friends.

For those seeking adventure, Madera Canyon boasts a network of well-maintained trails catering to all skill levels. From the easy-going Madera Canyon Nature Trail to the more challenging Mount Wrightson hike, there's something for everyone. The latter, a strenuous 10-mile round-trip trek, culminates in breathtaking panoramic views from the summit, rewarding hikers with an awe-inspiring vista of southern Arizona.

Madera Canyon isn't just a daytime destination; it also offers stargazing opportunities that are second to none. Due to its high elevation and minimal light pollution, the canyon provides an ideal setting for observing celestial wonders. Visitors often gather at the Proctor Road parking area to set up telescopes and revel in the brilliance of the night sky.

16. Titan Missile Museum

Situated in the desert landscape of southern Arizona, the Titan Missile Museum stands as a testament to the Cold War era and the intense rivalry between the United States and the Soviet Union. This unique museum offers visitors a rare opportunity to step into the underground world of a decommissioned Titan II intercontinental ballistic missile (ICBM) silo, providing a chilling glimpse into the era of nuclear deterrence and the delicate balance of power during the Cold War.

The Titan II missile system was a crucial component of the United States' nuclear arsenal during the Cold War. The museum's centerpiece is the preserved silo, complete with an actual Titan II missile. Visitors can descend into the underground control center, where they'll see the massive missile up close and learn about the complex launch procedures that were in place to ensure the nation's security.

The guided tours at the Titan Missile Museum are led by knowledgeable docents who provide historical context, technical insights, and firsthand accounts of the people who worked on the Titan II missile system. Visitors gain a deeper understanding of the strategic importance of these missiles and the profound impact they had on global geopolitics during the Cold War.

One of the most riveting moments of the tour is when visitors enter the control room and stand at the console where missile crews would have carried out their duties. The eerie authenticity of the control room, complete with vintage technology and period-specific furnishings, transports visitors back in time to an era of high-stakes tension and preparedness.

The museum also features exhibits and displays that explore the history of the Cold War, the arms race, and the broader cultural and political climate of the time. It sheds light on the efforts made to maintain peace through deterrence and the sacrifices of the individuals who served in these remote and secretive installations.

In addition to the historical and educational aspects, the Titan Missile Museum serves as a reminder of the importance of arms control and diplomacy in ensuring global stability. It prompts reflection on the consequences of nuclear conflict and the continued efforts to prevent it.

17. Colossal Cave Mountain Park

Nestled in the scenic Sonoran Desert of southern Arizona, Colossal Cave Mountain Park stands as a testament to nature's hidden marvels and the rich history of the American Southwest. This unique destination, located just a short drive from Tucson, offers visitors a captivating blend of geological wonders, outdoor adventures, and a glimpse into the past.

At the heart of the park lies Colossal Cave, a massive underground limestone cavern that has been millions of years in the making. Discovered by early Spanish explorers in the late 18th century, the cave system has since been a source of fascination for adventurers and curious minds alike. Guided tours through the cave's labyrinthine passages reveal stunning stalactites, stalagmites, flowstones, and other intricate formations that have formed over millennia. The temperature inside the cave remains a comfortable 70 degrees Fahrenheit year-round, making it an appealing escape from the desert heat in the summer and a cozy retreat during the cooler months.

Beyond the cave, Colossal Cave Mountain Park boasts a plethora of outdoor activities that cater to a wide range of interests and skill levels. The park's extensive trail system invites hikers, horseback riders, and mountain bikers to explore the rugged beauty of the Sonoran Desert. For those seeking a more leisurely experience, picnic areas are scattered throughout the park, providing a serene setting for a family gathering or a quiet meal amidst nature's splendor.

Adventurous spirits can also partake in activities such as rock climbing, guided horseback rides, and birdwatching, as the park is home to a diverse array of wildlife. From desert cottontails to Gila monsters, the park's inhabitants offer a glimpse into the region's unique ecosystem.

Colossal Cave Mountain Park is not just a natural wonderland; it also holds historical significance. The park is a testament to the resilience of early settlers who, in the late 1800s, used the cave as a refuge from the harsh desert elements. Visitors can explore the historic La Posta Quemada Ranch, which serves as a museum showcasing the area's history, offering a glimpse into the challenges and triumphs of those who lived here.

18. Pima Air & Space Museum

Located in Tucson, the Pima Air & Space Museum is an aviation enthusiast's dream and a treasure trove of aerospace history. Spread across 127 acres, this vast museum houses one of the most extensive collections of aircraft and space artifacts in the world, showcasing the evolution of flight and space exploration from the early days of aviation to the present.

The museum's outdoor "Aircraft Boneyard" is one of its most iconic features, where over 300 aircraft are displayed, including vintage warbirds, commercial airliners, experimental prototypes, and retired military planes. Walking among these colossal machines, visitors can gain a sense of the monumental advancements in aviation technology over the decades.

Inside the museum's hangars, visitors encounter a meticulously curated collection of aircraft and space artifacts that tell the story of human flight. The World War II Gallery, for example, houses legendary aircraft like the B-17 Flying Fortress and the P-51 Mustang, while the Space Gallery features artifacts from the early days of space exploration, including a Mercury space capsule and a full-scale mock-up of the Apollo lunar module.

One of the museum's standout attractions is the "390th Memorial Museum," which honors the history and sacrifices of the 390th Bomb Group, a World War II B-17 bomber unit. The museum features personal stories, artifacts, and exhibits that provide a poignant glimpse into the lives of the brave individuals who served during that era.

The Pima Air & Space Museum offers a variety of guided tours and educational programs for visitors of all ages. These programs delve into the science, technology, and history of aviation and space exploration, making it an excellent destination for families, students, and aviation enthusiasts.

For those seeking a more immersive experience, the museum offers the "Boneyard Tour," providing a guided tour of the nearby Davis-Monthan Air Force Base, where thousands of retired military aircraft are stored in the desert. It's a unique opportunity to witness aircraft preservation and the enormity of military aviation history.

19. Mission San Xavier del Bac

Mission San Xavier del Bac, often referred to as the "White Dove of the Desert," is a historical and architectural masterpiece located just south of Tucson, Arizona. This iconic Spanish mission, founded in 1692 by Jesuit missionary Father Eusebio Kino, is a symbol of both religious significance and cultural heritage.

The mission's stunning white facade, intricate carvings, and remarkable architecture blend European Baroque and Moorish styles, making it one of the finest examples of Spanish colonial architecture in the United States. The exterior is adorned with intricate sculptures and reliefs, reflecting the skilled craftsmanship of the indigenous O'odham people and the European artisans who worked on the mission.

As you approach the mission, you're greeted by the sight of two towering bell towers that reach toward the heavens, giving the impression of a majestic cathedral in the desert. The interior is equally awe-inspiring, with a nave adorned in richly detailed artwork and an altar that serves as the focal point for religious ceremonies.

San Xavier del Bac remains an active Catholic church, serving the Tohono O'odham Nation and the broader community. The mission continues to hold religious services and plays an essential role in the spiritual life of the region. Visitors are welcome to attend mass and experience the profound spiritual ambiance within the mission's walls.

Beyond its architectural and religious significance, Mission San Xavier del Bac is also a testament to the enduring relationship between the Catholic Church and the indigenous peoples of the Southwest. The mission's history is marked by cultural exchange, adaptation, and resilience, as the O'odham people embraced Catholicism while preserving their own traditions and way of life.

The mission has undergone extensive restoration efforts to ensure its preservation for future generations. The San Xavier Restoration Project has worked tirelessly to repair and maintain the mission's structure, allowing visitors to appreciate the intricate artwork, frescoes, and religious artifacts that adorn its interior.

Visitors to Mission San Xavier del Bac can explore the mission, learn about its history, and appreciate the deep spiritual and cultural significance it holds.

20. Tucson

Tucson, Arizona, is a vibrant and culturally rich city nestled in the Sonoran Desert, surrounded by breathtaking mountain ranges and stunning desert landscapes. Known for its sunny weather, diverse cultural heritage, and thriving arts scene, Tucson offers a unique blend of outdoor adventure, historical sites, and urban charm that attracts visitors year-round.

One of Tucson's most striking features is the surrounding natural beauty, with the Santa Catalina, Rincon, Tucson, and Santa Rita Mountains providing a picturesque backdrop. Outdoor enthusiasts can explore Saguaro National Park, which flanks the city on both the east and west sides and is home to towering saguaro cacti, scenic hiking trails, and incredible desert sunsets. Mount Lemmon, located in the Santa Catalina Mountains, offers a cool retreat from the desert heat with opportunities for hiking, rock climbing, and even skiing in the winter.

Tucson's rich cultural history is rooted in its Native American, Spanish, Mexican, and Old West influences, which are evident throughout the city. Historic sites like Mission San Xavier del Bac, an 18th-century Spanish colonial church, showcase stunning architecture and offer a glimpse into the region's past. Downtown Tucson features the Presidio San Agustín del Tucson, a reconstructed Spanish fort that tells the story of the city's early days.

The city is also known for its vibrant arts and culinary scenes. Tucson has been designated a UNESCO City of Gastronomy, thanks to its rich culinary heritage and the use of locally sourced ingredients. Visitors can savor delicious Southwestern cuisine, from traditional Mexican dishes to contemporary farm-to-table creations. The city's eclectic arts scene includes the Tucson Museum of Art, numerous galleries, and annual events like the Tucson Gem and Mineral Show, one of the largest of its kind in the world.

Whether you're exploring the rugged desert, experiencing the city's cultural and historical landmarks, or enjoying a vibrant meal at a local eatery, Tucson offers a unique blend of adventure, heritage, and charm. The city's diverse attractions make it a must-visit destination for travelers looking to experience the best of the American Southwest.

21. Old Tucson Studios

Nestled in the desert landscape of southern Arizona, Old Tucson Studios stands as a testament to the rich cinematic history of the American West. This iconic destination has played a significant role in the world of film and television, serving as the backdrop for numerous classic Western movies and television shows. Beyond its Hollywood legacy, Old Tucson Studios offers visitors a unique opportunity to step back in time and experience the Old West firsthand.

Founded in 1939, Old Tucson Studios has been the location for over 300 film and television productions, making it one of the most famous Western film sets in the world. Classic Westerns like "Gunfight at the O.K. Corral" (1957) and "Rio Bravo" (1959) were filmed on its dusty streets. The studio's rustic buildings, saloons, and wooden boardwalks create an authentic Old West atmosphere that has captured the imagination of filmmakers for generations.

Visitors to Old Tucson Studios can immerse themselves in this cinematic history through guided tours, live reenactments, and interactive shows. The park offers daily performances of gunfights, stunt shows, and musical acts, all set against the backdrop of its meticulously recreated Western town. These performances provide a thrilling glimpse into the action-packed world of the Wild West.

Beyond the entertainment, Old Tucson Studios also serves as a living history museum, where guests can explore the cultural heritage and daily life of the American frontier. The park features informative exhibits, historical artifacts, and costumed interpreters who bring the past to life. From the blacksmith's shop to the general store, visitors can step into the shoes of pioneers and gain a deeper understanding of the challenges they faced.

Old Tucson Studios is not just a tourist attraction; it's a living tribute to the Western film genre and a celebration of American history. Whether you're a film enthusiast, history buff, or simply looking for a unique and entertaining experience, a visit to Old Tucson Studios promises an unforgettable journey through the rugged and captivating world of the Old West. It's a place where the magic of the silver screen and the reality of the frontier blend seamlessly, offering a taste of the Wild West that continues to captivate audiences of all ages.

22. Arizona-Sonora Desert Museum

The Arizona-Sonora Desert Museum, located west of Tucson, is a world-renowned zoo, natural history museum, and botanical garden that offers an immersive experience of the Sonoran Desert. This unique institution, spread over 98 acres, provides visitors with an opportunity to explore the rich biodiversity of the desert in a single location.

Combining aspects of a zoo, museum, and garden, the Arizona-Sonora Desert Museum showcases over 230 animal species and 1,200 plant species native to the Sonoran Desert. The exhibits and habitats are designed to replicate the natural environment, providing visitors with a realistic and educational experience.

Key attractions at the museum include the walk-in aviary, where visitors can observe and interact with native birds; the hummingbird aviary, showcasing several species of these vibrant birds; and the reptile and invertebrate exhibits, displaying a variety of desert-dwelling creatures. The Mountain Woodland and Desert Grassland areas offer glimpses into the diverse ecosystems found within the Sonoran Desert.

The museum's botanical gardens feature a stunning array of desert plants, including an extensive collection of cacti and succulents. The gardens change with the seasons, offering a colorful display of wildflowers in the spring and a showcase of desert fruits and foliage in the fall.

In addition to its exhibits, the Arizona-Sonora Desert Museum is dedicated to conservation and education. It conducts research on desert ecology and provides a wide range of educational programs, including guided tours, animal demonstrations, and interactive activities for all ages.

23. Saguaro National Park

Saguaro National Park, located in the Sonoran Desert near Tucson, Arizona, is a breathtaking natural wonder that showcases the majestic saguaro cactus, the largest cactus species in the United States and an enduring symbol of the American Southwest. The park is split into two districts: the Rincon Mountain District to the east and the Tucson Mountain District to the west, both offering unique landscapes and opportunities to experience the incredible beauty of the desert environment.

The saguaro cactus, which can grow up to 50 feet tall and live for over 150 years, is the star attraction of the park. These iconic giants stand proudly across the desert landscape, creating a surreal and awe-inspiring scene, especially during sunrise and sunset when the sky is painted in vivid colors. In late spring, the saguaros bloom with beautiful white flowers, adding to the stunning desert scenery.

Saguaro National Park is a haven for outdoor enthusiasts, offering a variety of recreational activities. Hikers can explore more than 165 miles of trails that wind through diverse desert habitats, from scenic desert flats dotted with saguaros to rugged mountain trails with panoramic views of the surrounding landscape. The park's trails cater to all levels, from easy walks like the Desert Discovery Nature Trail to challenging hikes like the trek up to Wasson Peak, which offers breathtaking vistas of the Tucson basin.

The park is also rich in biodiversity, home to a wide variety of desert flora and fauna. Visitors may encounter wildlife such as javelinas, coyotes, desert tortoises, and a variety of bird species, including the Gila woodpecker and the cactus wren. The Rincon Mountain District features higher elevations and diverse plant communities, including oak and pine forests.

Visitors can learn about the park's unique ecosystem and the cultural significance of the saguaro cactus to Native American tribes at the visitor centers, which offer educational exhibits, guided tours, and ranger-led programs.

Saguaro National Park provides an unforgettable experience, immersing visitors in the stunning and serene beauty of the desert and offering a chance to marvel at the iconic saguaros that have come to define the rugged landscape of the American Southwest.

24. Catalina State Park

Catalina State Park, nestled at the base of the majestic Santa Catalina Mountains in southern Arizona, is a haven for outdoor enthusiasts and nature lovers. Spanning 5,500 acres of undisturbed Sonoran Desert landscapes, the park is located just north of Tucson and offers a diverse array of recreational opportunities and natural beauty.

This park is renowned for its stunning scenery, characterized by rugged trails, unique desert flora and fauna, and ancient Hohokam ruins. Visitors to Catalina State Park are greeted by a landscape dotted with massive saguaro cacti, mesquite trees, and a variety of desert shrubs and wildflowers. The park's varied elevation, ranging from 2,500 to 8,550 feet, contributes to its rich biodiversity.

One of the park's main attractions is its extensive trail system, boasting over 50 miles of trails for hiking, horseback riding, and mountain biking. These trails range from easy, family-friendly walks to challenging treks into the backcountry. The Romero Canyon Trail is a popular choice, leading hikers to a beautiful, seasonal waterfall and offering breathtaking views of the surrounding desert and canyons.

Birdwatching is another highlight at Catalina State Park, with over 150 bird species recorded in the area. The park's riparian corridors, like those along Sutherland Wash, attract an array of birdlife, making it a prime spot for bird enthusiasts. Wildlife sightings in the park may include javelinas, coyotes, bobcats, and various reptiles.

For those interested in archaeology, the park contains remnants of the ancient Hohokam civilization, including prehistoric rock art and ruins. The Romero Ruin Interpretive Trail offers an easy walk through a significant archaeological site in the park.

Catalina State Park also offers camping facilities, including sites for tents, trailers, and RVs, allowing visitors to experience the tranquil desert nights. The park hosts a variety of educational programs and guided hikes, enhancing the visitor experience with insights into the region's natural history and ecology.

25. Mount Lemmon

Mount Lemmon, located in the Santa Catalina Mountains just north of Tucson, Arizona, is a breathtaking destination that offers a refreshing escape from the desert heat and a diverse array of outdoor activities. Rising to an elevation of 9,159 feet, Mount Lemmon is the highest peak in the range and features a unique environment where visitors can experience a striking contrast between the arid desert below and the lush forests at the summit.

The drive up to Mount Lemmon, along the scenic Catalina Highway (also known as the Sky Island Scenic Byway), is an adventure in itself. The 27-mile route winds through several ecological zones, starting with the saguaro-studded desert and transitioning to oak and pine forests as you ascend. The journey offers breathtaking views and numerous pull-off points for photo opportunities, hiking, and picnicking. The changing landscapes make it feel like you're traveling through different climates and worlds in just a short distance.

Outdoor enthusiasts will find plenty to do on Mount Lemmon. The area is known for its extensive network of hiking and biking trails, with options for all skill levels. Popular trails include the Aspen Trail and Marshall Gulch, which offer stunning views of the surrounding mountains and forests. Rock climbers are drawn to Mount Lemmon's granite cliffs and boulders, which provide excellent climbing opportunities.

In the winter, Mount Lemmon transforms into a snowy wonderland and is home to the southernmost ski destination in the United States: the Mount Lemmon Ski Valley. Here, visitors can enjoy skiing, snowboarding, and other winter activities, making Mount Lemmon a year-round recreational hotspot.

The charming village of Summerhaven, located near the summit, offers cozy dining spots, unique shops, and cabin rentals, providing a perfect place to relax and take in the crisp mountain air. Popular stops include the Cookie Cabin, where you can indulge in giant, freshly baked cookies.

Mount Lemmon's stunning scenery, diverse activities, and refreshing climate make it a must-visit destination for anyone looking to explore the natural beauty of southern Arizona.

Eastern Arizona

1. **Rim Country Museum and Zane Grey Cabin**

The Rim Country Museum and Zane Grey Cabin, located in the charming town of Payson, offer a fascinating journey into the history, culture, and literary legacy of the region. This cultural complex celebrates the rich heritage of the Payson area and pays tribute to the famous author Zane Grey, who spent time in the region and was inspired by its natural beauty.

The Rim Country Museum is a treasure trove of artifacts, photographs, and exhibits that trace the history of Payson and the surrounding Rim Country. Visitors can explore displays on early settlers, ranching and mining, Native American culture, and the growth of the community. The museum's exhibits provide insights into the challenges and triumphs of the people who shaped the region's history.

One of the museum's standout features is the replica of a Western-style town street, complete with storefronts and period-appropriate displays. This immersive experience allows visitors to step back in time and get a feel for life in the Old West.

Adjacent to the museum is the historic Zane Grey Cabin, which served as the summer residence of the famous author Zane Grey. Grey, known for his Western novels and adventure stories, spent several summers in Payson during the 1920s and 1930s. The cabin has been preserved and offers a glimpse into the life of the prolific writer. Visitors can explore the cabin and its furnishings, as well as view exhibits on Zane Grey's life and work.

The Payson area, with its stunning landscapes and natural beauty, played a significant role in inspiring Zane Grey's writings. His love for the region is evident in his novels, many of which are set in the American West.

The museum complex also includes the Shoofly Village Ruin, an archaeological site that showcases the prehistoric history of the region. It offers visitors a chance to learn about the ancient cultures that once inhabited the area.

2. Mogollon Rim

The Mogollon Rim is a striking escarpment characterized by high cliffs, dense forests, and a diverse array of wildlife. The Rim, named after the ancient Mogollon culture, is not only a natural wonder but also a testament to the rich cultural history of the region.

Rising to an elevation of over 7,000 feet, the Mogollon Rim offers breathtaking panoramic views that are a feast for the eyes. Its topography is a dramatic shift from the lower, arid regions of Arizona, featuring lush ponderosa pine forests and numerous lakes and streams. This lush, highland environment provides a stark contrast to the desert landscapes typically associated with Arizona, showcasing the state's diverse ecological beauty.

The Mogollon Rim's climate and terrain make it a popular destination for outdoor enthusiasts. Hiking, camping, and fishing are some of the most popular activities. Trails such as the Rim Country Trails and the Highline Trail offer hikers varying levels of difficulty and the opportunity to explore the area's natural beauty. Campgrounds scattered along the Rim provide opportunities for overnight stays, where visitors can immerse themselves in the tranquility of nature. The Rim's lakes and streams, teeming with trout and other fish, are a haven for anglers.

For wildlife enthusiasts and photographers, the Mogollon Rim is a living gallery. It is home to an array of wildlife, including elk, deer, black bears, and a multitude of bird species. The diversity of habitats along the Rim supports a rich variety of flora and fauna, making it a prime spot for nature observation and photography.

The Rim is also steeped in history. It was a significant territory for the Mogollon culture, an ancient Native American group, and later for the Apache and Yavapai peoples. Throughout the area, one can find traces of these cultures in the form of ancient dwellings, pottery shards, and other artifacts. Additionally, the Rim played a crucial role in the westward expansion of the United States, with settlers and pioneers traversing its challenging terrain.

Today, the Mogollon Rim is not only an outdoor paradise but also a vital natural resource. It forms a significant part of the watershed for central Arizona, contributing to the region's water supply. Its forests are critical in maintaining the ecological balance and biodiversity of the area.

3. Fool Hollow Lake Recreation Area

Tucked away in the picturesque White Mountains of eastern Arizona, Fool Hollow Lake Recreation Area is a haven for outdoor enthusiasts and nature lovers. This pristine destination is centered around a tranquil 150-acre lake, surrounded by dense forests, offering a wide range of recreational activities and a serene escape from the desert heat.

Fool Hollow Lake is the main attraction of the recreation area, known for its clear, cool waters and the opportunity for boating, fishing, and swimming. Anglers flock to the lake to catch a variety of fish, including rainbow trout, bass, and catfish. The well-maintained boat ramps and marina make it easy for visitors to launch their watercraft, and fishing piers are accessible for those who prefer to fish from the shore.

The recreation area offers a diverse network of hiking and biking trails that wind through the surrounding pine and oak forests. These trails provide excellent opportunities for birdwatching, as the area is home to a wide range of bird species. Ospreys, bald eagles, and a variety of waterfowl can be spotted around the lake.

Fool Hollow Lake Recreation Area boasts a family-friendly atmosphere, with a sandy swimming beach and a playground for children. Picnic areas with barbecue grills and picnic tables are available, making it an ideal spot for a lakeside picnic with family and friends.

For those seeking overnight accommodations, the recreation area offers a campground with a mix of RV and tent sites. Some sites are located directly on the lake's shore, providing stunning views and a serene atmosphere for camping under the stars. Additionally, the park has modern restrooms and showers, making it a comfortable and convenient destination for extended stays.

The beauty of Fool Hollow Lake Recreation Area is not limited to the summer months. During the fall, the surrounding forests burst into vibrant autumn colors, creating a picturesque landscape that attracts photographers and leaf-peepers. In the winter, the area transforms into a snowy wonderland, inviting cross-country skiers and snowshoers to explore the quiet trails.

4. Show Low

Show Low, a picturesque city nestled in the White Mountains of eastern Arizona, is a vibrant and welcoming community that offers a unique blend of outdoor adventures, cultural attractions, and a rich history. Named after a legendary card game, Show Low beckons visitors with its beautiful landscapes and a wide range of recreational activities.

The city's most iconic feature is the Show Low Deuce of Clubs, a distinctively shaped mountain that overlooks the town. Its name is a nod to the legend of how the city got its name. According to the tale, two early settlers, Corydon E. Cooley and Marion Clark, played a game of poker to determine who would name the newly settled town. Cooley reportedly said, "If you can show low, you win," and showed the deuce of clubs, thus naming the town.

Show Low offers a wealth of outdoor activities year-round. The nearby Apache-Sitgreaves National Forests provide hiking and biking trails that wind through the scenic wilderness, allowing visitors to explore the dense pine forests and encounter wildlife such as elk, deer, and a variety of bird species.

Fool Hollow Lake Recreation Area, located just a short drive from Show Low, is a popular destination for boating, fishing, and picnicking. The serene lake offers opportunities for kayaking, canoeing, and paddleboarding, and anglers can try their luck at catching a variety of fish, including trout and bass.

During the winter months, Show Low becomes a snowy paradise, drawing winter sports enthusiasts to the Sunrise Park Resort. The resort offers excellent downhill skiing and snowboarding terrain, as well as groomed cross-country skiing trails.

Show Low's downtown district boasts a charming mix of shops, restaurants, and cultural attractions. The Show Low Historical Society Museum showcases the area's rich history, with exhibits on early settlers, Native American heritage, and the city's unique name origin.

The city also hosts a variety of events and festivals throughout the year, including the annual Show Low Days celebration, which features a parade, live music, and family-friendly activities.

5. Pinetop-Lakeside

Nestled in the heart of Arizona's White Mountains, Pinetop-Lakeside is a serene and picturesque mountain town that beckons visitors with its cool climate, lush forests, and a wide range of outdoor activities. This charming community is a year-round destination, offering a respite from the desert heat and a chance to immerse oneself in nature's beauty.

Surrounded by the Apache-Sitgreaves National Forests, Pinetop-Lakeside is a haven for outdoor enthusiasts. Hiking, mountain biking, and horseback riding are popular activities on the numerous trails that wind through the dense pine and oak forests. The White Mountains Trail System offers a network of interconnected trails that cater to hikers of all skill levels.

During the summer months, the region's many lakes provide opportunities for boating, fishing, and water sports. Woodland Lake Park and Rainbow Lake are two popular spots for fishing and picnicking, offering scenic views and a peaceful ambiance.

In the winter, Pinetop-Lakeside transforms into a snowy wonderland, drawing skiers, snowboarders, and snowshoers to nearby Sunrise Park Resort. The resort offers excellent downhill skiing and snowboarding terrain, as well as groomed cross-country skiing trails.

Pinetop-Lakeside also boasts a thriving arts and culture scene, with local galleries, theaters, and music venues that showcase the talents of the community. The Hon-Dah Resort Casino and Conference Center provides entertainment and gaming options for those seeking indoor activities.

For golf enthusiasts, the area is home to several golf courses, including the Pinetop Lakes Golf and Country Club, which offers scenic fairways and a challenging round of golf amidst the mountain backdrop.

The town hosts a variety of events and festivals throughout the year, celebrating everything from art and music to the natural beauty of the White Mountains. The Cool Mountain Triathlon, the Woodland Wildlife and Outdoor Expo, and the High Mountain Music Festival are just a few examples of the community gatherings that bring residents and visitors together.

Whether you're seeking outdoor adventure, cultural enrichment, or simply a tranquil mountain escape, Pinetop-Lakeside offers a warm and welcoming atmosphere in a pristine natural setting.

6. Kinishba Ruins

Kinishba Ruins, located near the town of Whiteriver in eastern Arizona, is a remarkable archaeological site that offers a glimpse into the ancient history and culture of the Indigenous people who once inhabited the region. This well-preserved site is a testament to the architectural and engineering achievements of the ancestral Puebloans, also known as the Ancestral Hopi.

The ruins are situated on the Fort Apache Indian Reservation and are part of the White Mountain Apache Tribe's cultural heritage. Kinishba, meaning "Brown House" in Apache, is a complex of pueblo-style buildings constructed between 1250 and 1350 AD. It is believed to have been an important center for the Ancestral Hopi people, serving as both a ceremonial site and a place for community gatherings.

One of the most striking features of Kinishba Ruins is the large, multi-story pueblo structure known as the Great House. This architectural marvel is made up of hundreds of rooms, kivas (ceremonial chambers), and plazas. The Great House is a testament to the advanced engineering and construction techniques of the Ancestral Hopi, with its walls made of stone and adobe mortar.

Visitors to Kinishba Ruins can explore the site through guided tours offered by the White Mountain Apache Tribe's Cultural Center and Museum. Knowledgeable guides provide insights into the history, architecture, and significance of the ruins, as well as the cultural heritage of the Apache people. The tour also includes a visit to the nearby Kinishba Museum, which features exhibits on the history and culture of the White Mountain Apache Tribe.

In addition to its historical and cultural significance, Kinishba Ruins offers a scenic and tranquil environment. Surrounded by the natural beauty of the White Mountains and the Apache-Sitgreaves National Forests, the site provides an opportunity for reflection and appreciation of the region's rich heritage.

Kinishba Ruins stands as a testament to the enduring legacy of the Ancestral Hopi and the importance of preserving and celebrating the cultural heritage of Indigenous communities. It is a place where visitors can connect with the past, gain a deeper understanding of the ancient cultures of the American Southwest, and appreciate the significance of the site to the White Mountain Apache Tribe.

7. Fort Apache Historic Park

Nestled in the heart of the White Mountains of eastern Arizona, Fort Apache Historic Park is a living testament to the history and culture of the Apache people and the United States military in the American Southwest. This historic site preserves the remains of an old military fort and provides insights into the complex interactions between Indigenous tribes and the U.S. government during the late 19th and early 20th centuries.

Originally established as a military outpost in 1870, Fort Apache played a pivotal role in the Indian Wars of the late 19th century. It was home to the famous African American "Buffalo Soldiers" and served as a base for campaigns against the Apache tribes. The fort's history is intricately tied to the Apache Wars and the tumultuous period of westward expansion in the United States.

Today, Fort Apache Historic Park offers a glimpse into the past with well-preserved historic buildings, including officer's quarters, enlisted men's barracks, and a historic cemetery. The White Mountain Apache Tribe operates the site and has transformed it into a living history museum.

Visitors can explore the park through self-guided tours or with knowledgeable guides who provide insights into the history and culture of the Apache people. The Kinishba Ruins and Archaeological Site, located nearby, offer further opportunities to learn about the ancient history of the region and the ancestral lands of the Apache Tribe.

The park also hosts cultural events and celebrations, including the annual Fort Apache Heritage Days, which feature traditional Apache dances, arts and crafts, and cultural demonstrations. These events provide a unique opportunity to experience the rich heritage of the Apache people.

The scenic beauty of the White Mountains serves as a backdrop to the historic site, offering opportunities for hiking, birdwatching, and wildlife viewing. The park's visitor center provides educational exhibits and a gift shop where visitors can purchase handmade crafts created by members of the White Mountain Apache Tribe.

8. White Mountains

The White Mountains of Arizona offer a serene and picturesque escape from the heat and bustle of the desert southwest. Located in the eastern part of the state, this region is renowned for its lush forests, crystal-clear lakes, and diverse outdoor recreational opportunities. Covering approximately 2,900 square miles, the White Mountains are part of the larger Colorado Plateau and are an oasis of natural beauty.

One of the most striking features of the White Mountains is its dense pine forests, which include the largest stand of ponderosa pines in the world. The towering trees provide a cool respite during the summer months and offer a dramatic contrast to the arid landscapes found elsewhere in Arizona. Exploring the network of hiking and biking trails allows visitors to immerse themselves in the serene forest environment, with opportunities to spot wildlife such as elk, deer, and a variety of bird species.

The White Mountains are home to a number of pristine lakes, making it a popular destination for fishing, boating, and water sports. Lakes like Big Lake, Luna Lake, and Hawley Lake are ideal for anglers seeking trout, bass, and catfish. Many of these lakes offer camping facilities, allowing visitors to enjoy the beauty of the area's night skies and the soothing sounds of nature.

During the fall season, the White Mountains come alive with vibrant autumn colors as the leaves of aspen and maple trees turn shades of gold and crimson. This natural spectacle draws photographers, leaf-peepers, and nature enthusiasts to witness the stunning transformation of the landscape.

The Apache-Sitgreaves National Forests, which encompass much of the White Mountains, provide a range of recreational opportunities, including camping, picnicking, and wildlife viewing. The forests are crisscrossed with scenic byways and trails that lead to viewpoints, waterfalls, and remote wilderness areas, making it a paradise for outdoor adventurers.

The region also boasts a rich history, with evidence of prehistoric Native American cultures and early pioneer settlements. The White Mountains Historical Society and local museums offer insights into the area's past and the people who shaped its history.

9. Greer

Greer, is a charming and idyllic mountain town nestled in the heart of the White Mountains. Known for its pristine natural beauty, cool climate, and friendly community, Greer is a year-round destination that offers a retreat from the hustle and bustle of city life.

Surrounded by lush forests, the town of Greer is an outdoor enthusiast's paradise. In the summer, visitors can enjoy hiking, mountain biking, and horseback riding on the area's scenic trails. The Little Colorado River flows through Greer, providing excellent opportunities for fishing and wildlife viewing.

The town is also a hub for birdwatching, with a wide range of species calling the White Mountains home. Bird enthusiasts can spot hummingbirds, tanagers, and various woodpeckers while exploring the area's serene forests.

During the fall, Greer becomes a vibrant tapestry of autumn colors as the leaves of aspen and maple trees turn brilliant shades of gold and crimson. This seasonal display attracts photographers, nature lovers, and those seeking a peaceful escape in the midst of nature's beauty.

In the winter, Greer transforms into a snowy wonderland, making it a prime destination for winter sports and recreation. Cross-country skiing, snowshoeing, and snowmobiling are popular activities in the surrounding wilderness areas.

One of the town's standout features is the Little Colorado River Greer Trout Hatchery, where visitors can learn about the process of raising trout and even feed the fish. Greer is known for its excellent trout fishing, with the Little Colorado River and nearby lakes providing ample opportunities to cast a line.

Greer offers a range of accommodation options, including cozy cabins, bed and breakfasts, and vacation rentals. Many of these lodgings feature stunning mountain views and a peaceful ambiance that makes them ideal for a restful getaway.

The town also hosts various events and festivals throughout the year, celebrating the seasons and the community's rich heritage. The annual Greer Days event, held in the summer, features a parade, live music, and family-friendly activities that bring the town together.

10. Butterfly Lodge Museum

The Butterfly Lodge Museum, located in the picturesque White Mountains of Arizona, is a charming historical site that offers a glimpse into the early 20th-century American literary scene. This museum was once the summer home of James Willard Schultz, a noted author and explorer, and his son, Hart Merriam Schultz, an artist known for his Native American themes.

The lodge, built in 1913, is a beautiful example of early American log cabin architecture. Its rustic exterior and cozy interior create a warm and inviting atmosphere. The museum houses an extensive collection of artifacts and memorabilia related to the life and work of Schultz and his son. These include original manuscripts, letters, photographs, and artworks, providing an intimate look at their creative processes and personal lives.

Visitors to the Butterfly Lodge Museum can embark on guided tours, where they can learn about the historical and cultural significance of the lodge and its former inhabitants. The tours also highlight the influence of Native American culture on Schultz's writing and his son's art, offering insights into the cultural interactions of that era.

The museum is not just a tribute to two remarkable individuals; it's a celebration of the rich cultural tapestry of the American West. It provides a unique perspective on the artistic and literary movements of the early 20th century, as well as the ongoing influence of Native American culture.

Set against the backdrop of the stunning White Mountains, the Butterfly Lodge Museum is a peaceful retreat that allows visitors to step back in time and experience a slice of American history. Its combination of natural beauty, historical significance, and cultural richness makes it a unique and enriching destination.

11. X Diamond Ranch

X Diamond Ranch offers a unique blend of natural beauty and rich history. This ranch, spanning several acres, is a paradise for those seeking a serene getaway or an adventurous outdoor experience.

The ranch's history is deeply intertwined with the development of the American West. Originally established in the late 19th century, it has witnessed the evolution of the region from a wild frontier to a modern hub of outdoor recreation and conservation. The X Diamond Ranch has been carefully preserved, maintaining its rustic charm and historical significance.

Visitors to the ranch can indulge in a variety of activities. Horseback riding is a popular choice, allowing guests to explore the vast expanses of the property and its surrounding areas. The trails meander through scenic landscapes, offering breathtaking views of the Arizona wilderness. For fishing enthusiasts, the ranch boasts well-stocked ponds and streams, providing a peaceful and rewarding fishing experience.

Wildlife viewing is another highlight at X Diamond Ranch. The area is home to a diverse array of wildlife, including elk, deer, and a variety of bird species. Nature lovers and photographers will find plenty of opportunities to observe and capture the beauty of these creatures in their natural habitat.

The ranch also offers accommodations for those wishing to extend their stay. From cozy cabins to luxurious lodges, there is a range of options to suit different preferences and budgets. These accommodations are designed to provide comfort and tranquility, allowing guests to fully immerse themselves in the natural beauty of the ranch.

X Diamond Ranch is not just a destination; it's an experience that combines adventure, relaxation, and a journey through the rich tapestry of American history.

12. Lyman Lake State Park

Lyman Lake State Park, located in eastern Arizona, is a hidden oasis in the arid landscape of the Southwest. Nestled amidst the high desert terrain, this reservoir is the largest in the state and offers a wide range of recreational opportunities, making it a popular destination for outdoor enthusiasts and families alike.

The centerpiece of Lyman Lake State Park is the 1,500-acre reservoir, surrounded by scenic desert landscapes and framed by the distant peaks of the White Mountains. The lake provides a picturesque setting for boating, fishing, and water sports. Anglers can try their luck at catching a variety of fish, including largemouth bass, channel catfish, and walleye.

Boating and water skiing are popular activities on the lake, and the park offers a marina with boat rentals for those without their own watercraft. Kayaking and paddleboarding are also enjoyable ways to explore the calm waters of Lyman Lake.

The park offers numerous campsites, including sites with full hook-ups for RVs and more primitive sites for tent camping. Camping at Lyman Lake allows visitors to fully immerse themselves in the serene desert surroundings and enjoy the starry night skies.

Hiking and nature trails wind through the park, offering opportunities for wildlife viewing and birdwatching. The diverse desert landscape is home to a variety of wildlife, including mule deer, javelinas, and a wide range of bird species.

For those interested in history, the park features a visitor center that provides insights into the area's cultural and natural history. The nearby Lyman Lake Petroglyph Site offers a chance to view ancient petroglyphs etched into rocks by Indigenous people.

Lyman Lake State Park is a peaceful retreat where visitors can escape the hustle and bustle of urban life and unwind in the tranquil beauty of the Arizona desert. Whether you're boating on the lake, hiking the trails, or simply relaxing by the water, Lyman Lake offers a welcome respite in a remote and scenic corner of the state.

13. Eagar

Eagar, a charming town located in Arizona's White Mountains, is a hidden gem that offers a blend of small-town charm, natural beauty, and outdoor adventures. With its scenic surroundings and a strong sense of community, Eagar provides a tranquil escape for visitors seeking a refreshing mountain retreat.

Nestled at an elevation of over 7,000 feet, Eagar boasts a cool climate, making it an ideal destination to escape the Arizona desert heat during the summer months. The town is surrounded by the Apache-Sitgreaves National Forests, offering a wealth of outdoor activities year-round.

Hiking and mountain biking enthusiasts will find a variety of trails that wind through the nearby forests, showcasing the lush pine and fir landscapes. These trails provide opportunities for exploration and wildlife viewing, with the chance to spot elk, deer, and a diverse range of bird species.

Eagar is a gateway to the renowned White Mountains Trail System, a network of interconnected trails that cater to hikers and bikers of all skill levels. This system allows visitors to immerse themselves in the pristine wilderness and experience the region's natural beauty.

The nearby Little Colorado River is a popular spot for fishing, and the area's clear waters provide excellent opportunities to catch a variety of trout species. Anglers can cast their lines into the tranquil river while surrounded by the serene beauty of the high country.

During the winter, Eagar transforms into a snowy wonderland, drawing winter sports enthusiasts to the nearby Sunrise Park Resort. The resort offers downhill skiing, snowboarding, and snow tubing, providing a thrilling winter experience for visitors of all ages.

Eagar also celebrates its heritage and culture through local events and festivals. The annual Eagar Days event, featuring a parade, live music, and community gatherings, is a testament to the town's strong sense of community and pride.

For those interested in history, the Eagar Historical Museum offers insights into the town's past and showcases artifacts and exhibits that highlight its development and the lives of its early settlers.

14. Springerville Heritage Center

The Springerville Heritage Center, located in the heart of Springerville, is a cultural and historical hub that offers visitors a fascinating glimpse into the rich heritage of the region. Housed in a beautifully restored historic building, the center serves as a focal point for preserving, celebrating, and sharing the history and culture of Springerville and the surrounding area.

The center's exhibits showcase the history of the town, from its early days as a trading post to its growth as a thriving community in the late 19th and early 20th centuries. Visitors can explore displays of artifacts, photographs, and documents that provide insights into the lives of the town's pioneers, ranchers, and Native American communities.

One of the highlights of the Springerville Heritage Center is the Native American Gallery, which pays tribute to the Indigenous people of the region. The gallery features traditional art, crafts, and historical information about the Apache and Navajo tribes that have deep roots in the area.

The center also hosts rotating exhibits and special events that highlight different aspects of the region's history and culture. These events often include lectures, workshops, and presentations by local historians and experts.

The beautifully restored building that houses the Springerville Heritage Center is a historical treasure in itself. Originally constructed in 1892, the building has served various purposes over the years, including as a school and a community center. Its architecture reflects the Victorian-era style of the late 19th century and adds to the center's charm.

In addition to its exhibitions and events, the Springerville Heritage Center also houses a gift shop where visitors can purchase unique locally made crafts, books on regional history, and souvenirs that celebrate the heritage of the area.

The center serves as a focal point for the community, bringing residents together to celebrate their shared history and culture. It also provides educational opportunities for schools and visitors from near and far, helping to preserve and pass on the stories and traditions of the White Mountains.

15. Casa Malpais Archaeological Park

Casa Malpais Archaeological Park, located in Springerville, is a fascinating window into the past, offering insights into the lives of the Mogollon people who inhabited the region centuries ago. This site is renowned for its well-preserved ruins and ancient artifacts, making it a must-visit destination for history buffs and archaeology enthusiasts.

The park features a remarkable array of archaeological structures, including a Great Kiva, an ancient ceremonial structure unique to the cultures of the American Southwest. Visitors can explore these ruins and marvel at the ingenuity and craftsmanship of the Mogollon people. The site also boasts a series of ancient stairways and rock art, which provide a glimpse into the spiritual and daily lives of the early inhabitants.

Guided tours are available, offering in-depth information about the history, culture, and architecture of the site. These tours are led by knowledgeable guides who bring the history of Casa Malpais to life, making it an educational and engaging experience.

In addition to its archaeological significance, the park is situated in a stunning natural setting. The surrounding landscape, characterized by rugged cliffs and lush vegetation, adds to the mystical ambiance of the site. Visitors can enjoy the scenic beauty while pondering the mysteries of the past.

Casa Malpais Archaeological Park serves as a vital link to the ancient history of the American Southwest, providing a unique opportunity to connect with the past and appreciate the rich cultural heritage of the region.

16. Sipe White Mountain Wildlife Area

Nestled in the verdant expanses of Eastern Arizona's White Mountains, the Sipe White Mountain Wildlife Area is an enchanting destination that beckons nature lovers, hikers, and anyone with an appreciation for the serene beauty of the natural world. This sprawling wildlife haven, covering over 1,362 acres, is a testament to Arizona's commitment to preserving its natural heritage and offering a sanctuary for both wildlife and human visitors alike.

The Sipe White Mountain Wildlife Area, managed by the Arizona Game and Fish Department, is strategically positioned near the town of Eagar, making it an accessible retreat from the hustle and bustle of city life. The area's diverse ecosystem, characterized by lush meadows, riparian wetlands, and dense forests of ponderosa pines, provides a habitat for an array of wildlife, including elk, mule deer, and numerous bird species such as eagles, ospreys, and songbirds. It's a place where the silence is broken only by the sounds of nature: the rustling of leaves, the calls of birds, and the gentle flow of water.

For those inclined to explore, Sipe offers a network of trails that wind through its varied landscapes. These trails are not just pathways through the wilderness; they are gateways to discovery, offering breathtaking views, encounters with wildlife, and the tranquility that comes from being surrounded by nature. Each season brings its own unique beauty and opportunities for outdoor activities, from wildflower viewing in the spring to vibrant autumn colors that transform the landscape.

Beyond its natural allure, Sipe White Mountain Wildlife Area is steeped in history. Visitors can explore the remnants of the old Sipe homestead, which provides a glimpse into the area's past and the pioneers who once called this land home. This historical aspect adds depth to the visitor experience, connecting the past with the present in a setting that has remained largely untouched by time.

Educational opportunities abound, with interpretive signage along the trails providing insights into the area's ecology, wildlife species, and conservation efforts. These educational elements make Sipe not just a destination for recreation, but a place for learning and reflection on the importance of preserving natural habitats.

17. Big Lake

This expansive natural lake, located at an elevation of over 9,000 feet, offers a peaceful escape from the desert heat and a chance to immerse oneself in the pristine beauty of the high country.

Big Lake is the centerpiece of the Big Lake Recreation Area, which encompasses several lakeside campgrounds and a variety of outdoor recreational opportunities. The lake itself covers approximately 450 acres and is surrounded by dense pine forests, creating a tranquil and scenic environment.

One of the primary draws of Big Lake is its excellent fishing. The lake is known for its abundance of trout, including rainbow, cutthroat, and brook trout. Anglers of all skill levels can enjoy fishing from the shore, from a boat, or while wading in the clear waters. The lake is stocked regularly, ensuring a steady supply of eager fish.

Boating and water sports are popular on Big Lake, with opportunities for kayaking, canoeing, and sailing. A boat ramp provides easy access for those with their watercraft, and rentals are available for visitors who want to explore the lake's scenic coves and inlets.

Surrounding the lake, a network of hiking and biking trails winds through the forests, offering opportunities to spot wildlife such as elk, deer, and a variety of bird species. Birdwatchers will delight in the chance to observe ospreys, bald eagles, and other avian residents.

Camping at Big Lake is a tranquil experience, with campgrounds offering a range of amenities from basic tent sites to sites with full RV hook-ups. Many campgrounds are situated directly along the lake's shore, providing breathtaking views and the soothing sounds of nature. The cool mountain air and starry night skies make for an ideal camping getaway.

During the fall, Big Lake comes alive with vibrant autumn colors as the leaves of aspen and maple trees turn shades of gold and crimson. This natural spectacle draws photographers, leaf-peepers, and nature enthusiasts to witness the stunning transformation of the landscape.

In the winter, Big Lake is typically blanketed in snow, creating a serene and picturesque winter wonderland. The area becomes a playground for cross-country skiers and snowshoers, with trails winding through the snowy forests.

18. Coronado Trail Scenic Byway

The Coronado Trail Scenic Byway, also known as U.S. Route 191, is a breathtaking journey through the heart of Arizona's White Mountains, offering travelers a stunning and diverse array of landscapes, wildlife, and outdoor adventures. This 120-mile stretch of highway takes you from Clifton in the south to Springerville in the north, following the path once traveled by the Spanish explorer Francisco Vázquez de Coronado in the 16th century.

The byway meanders through some of Arizona's most remote and rugged terrain, passing through high mountain forests, deep canyons, and picturesque valleys. Along the way, you'll be treated to panoramic vistas, pristine wilderness, and a chance to experience the rich history and culture of the region.

One of the highlights of the Coronado Trail is the Gila Box Riparian National Conservation Area, where the Gila River winds through dramatic canyons, providing a haven for birdwatchers, hikers, and kayakers. The area is home to a wide variety of wildlife, including bald eagles, desert bighorn sheep, and river otters.

The byway also passes near the town of Clifton, where you can explore the historic Coronado Trail Interpretive Center, offering insights into the history of the area and the adventures of the Spanish explorers.

As you ascend into the higher elevations, you'll reach Hannagan Meadow, a pristine mountain meadow surrounded by pine forests. It's an excellent spot for a picnic or a hike, and during the winter, it transforms into a snowy wonderland for cross-country skiing and snowshoeing.

The Coronado Trail Scenic Byway is known for its winding, mountainous roads and hairpin turns, making it a thrilling drive for those who love a bit of adventure. However, be prepared for rapidly changing weather conditions, especially at higher elevations, as the route can be impassable during winter storms.

The journey along the Coronado Trail Scenic Byway is not just about the destination; it's about the breathtaking landscapes and the sense of awe that comes from exploring this remote and pristine corner of Arizona. Whether you're an outdoor enthusiast, a history buff, or simply seeking a scenic drive through nature's wonderland, the Coronado Trail promises an unforgettable experience.

19. Alpine

Alpine is a charming mountain town nestled in the White Mountains and is renowned for its stunning natural beauty, outdoor recreation, and vibrant arts scene. Situated at an elevation of over 8,000 feet, Alpine offers a refreshing escape from the desert heat and a unique blend of small-town charm and alpine adventure.

The town is surrounded by the Apache-Sitgreaves National Forests, providing a wealth of outdoor activities year-round. Hiking and mountain biking trails wind through the dense pine and fir forests, offering opportunities to explore the lush mountain landscapes and spot wildlife, including elk, deer, and a variety of bird species.

The San Francisco River, which runs through Alpine, is a popular spot for fishing and birdwatching. The area's clear streams and rivers provide excellent trout fishing, attracting anglers from far and wide. Bird enthusiasts will appreciate the chance to spot hummingbirds, tanagers, and various woodpeckers while exploring the surrounding wilderness.

During the winter months, Alpine becomes a snowy paradise, making it a prime destination for winter sports and recreation. Cross-country skiing, snowshoeing, and snowmobiling are popular activities in the nearby wilderness areas, offering a serene and peaceful experience in the winter wonderland.

Alpine's vibrant arts scene is celebrated throughout the year with art festivals, galleries, and cultural events. The town hosts the Annual Alpine Artwalk, where local and regional artists showcase their work in a charming mountain setting.

Alpine also boasts a strong sense of community, with events like the Alpine Area Historical Association's Pioneer Days and the Alpine Country Fair bringing residents and visitors together to celebrate the town's history and culture.

The town's location on the Coronado Trail Scenic Byway offers easy access to the dramatic landscapes and outdoor adventures of the surrounding region. Visitors can explore the nearby Hannagan Meadow, a pristine mountain meadow surrounded by pine forests and an excellent spot for hiking and picnicking.

Alpine's friendly atmosphere and natural beauty make it an ideal destination for those seeking a tranquil mountain escape.

20. Apache-Sitgreaves National Forests

The Apache-Sitgreaves National Forests, located in east-central Arizona, encompass over 2 million acres of pristine wilderness, offering a haven for outdoor enthusiasts and nature lovers. These two national forests, named after the Apache and Sitgreaves National Forest Reserves, are known for their diverse landscapes, abundant wildlife, and recreational opportunities that span all seasons.

The forests feature a wide range of ecosystems, from the high-elevation pine forests of the White Mountains to the arid canyons of the Mogollon Rim. This diversity makes the Apache-Sitgreaves National Forests a paradise for hikers, campers, anglers, hunters, and wildlife enthusiasts.

The White Mountains, within the forests' boundaries, are home to a dense stand of ponderosa pines and numerous lakes and streams. These pristine waters provide excellent fishing for trout, bass, and catfish, attracting anglers from far and wide. Hiking and camping opportunities abound, with numerous campgrounds and backcountry trails that allow visitors to explore the rugged terrain, discover waterfalls, and witness the stunning seasonal changes.

The Mogollon Rim, a dramatic geological feature, marks the southern edge of the Colorado Plateau and offers breathtaking vistas of forested plateaus and deep canyons. The Apache-Sitgreaves National Forests provide access to the rim's edge, where visitors can hike along the rim trails or enjoy panoramic views from overlooks such as the popular Mogollon Rim Visitor Center.

Wildlife is abundant in the forests, with opportunities for birdwatching and wildlife photography. The region is home to elk, deer, black bears, and a variety of bird species, making it a prime destination for observing and appreciating the natural world.

During the winter months, the forests transform into a snowy wonderland, drawing snowshoers, cross-country skiers, and snowmobilers. The Apache-Sitgreaves National Forests offer a tranquil and picturesque setting for those seeking winter recreation.

For those interested in exploring the forests' rich history, there are remnants of early pioneer settlements, historic cabins, and evidence of prehistoric Native American cultures. The area's cultural heritage is showcased in local museums and historical sites.

21. Hannagan Meadow

Hannagan Meadow, situated in the heart of Arizona's White Mountains, is a serene and picturesque high-elevation destination that offers a tranquil escape from the hustle and bustle of urban life. This pristine mountain meadow, located at an elevation of over 9,000 feet, is surrounded by dense pine forests and provides a breathtaking natural setting for outdoor enthusiasts and nature lovers.

The meadow itself is a lush, open expanse that comes alive with wildflowers during the spring and summer months. Visitors can enjoy picnics, relaxation, and leisurely walks amidst the vibrant colors of the meadow. It's an ideal spot for capturing the beauty of the White Mountains through photography or simply unwinding in a serene environment.

Hannagan Meadow is also a gateway to a network of hiking trails that wind through the surrounding wilderness. These trails offer opportunities for exploration and wildlife viewing, with the chance to encounter elk, deer, and a variety of bird species.

The meadow is a popular starting point for hiking adventures in the region, including the scenic Blue Range Primitive Area and the Blue Range Wilderness, which provide miles of trails through diverse landscapes, from pine forests to rugged canyons.

During the fall, Hannagan Meadow becomes a vibrant tapestry of autumn colors as the leaves of aspen and maple trees turn brilliant shades of gold and crimson. This seasonal display attracts photographers, leaf-peepers, and nature enthusiasts who come to witness the stunning transformation of the landscape.

Hannagan Meadow offers a range of accommodations for those looking to extend their stay in this mountain paradise. The Hannagan Meadow Lodge provides rustic and cozy lodging options, including cabins and rooms in a charming mountain lodge. These accommodations offer a comfortable and convenient base for exploring the surrounding wilderness.

The area is also known for its clear night skies, making it a prime destination for stargazing. On clear nights, visitors can enjoy unparalleled views of the Milky Way and celestial wonders.

22. Blue Range Primitive Area

Nestled in the remote and rugged mountains of eastern Arizona and western New Mexico, the Blue Range Primitive Area is a pristine wilderness that beckons adventurers seeking solitude and a genuine backcountry experience. Covering over 173,000 acres, this protected area is known for its untouched landscapes, diverse ecosystems, and abundant wildlife.

The Blue Range Primitive Area is part of the larger Apache-Sitgreaves National Forests, and its isolation and limited access contribute to its pristine condition. Visitors can explore this untouched wilderness by hiking along the numerous trails that crisscross the area, offering opportunities for both day hikes and extended backpacking adventures.

One of the standout features of the Blue Range Primitive Area is its biodiversity. The area encompasses a variety of ecosystems, from pine forests to high-elevation meadows and lush riparian zones. This diversity provides habitat for a wide range of wildlife, including elk, deer, black bears, mountain lions, and numerous bird species. Birdwatchers will appreciate the chance to spot rare and elusive species in this remote wilderness.

The Blue Range Wilderness is renowned for its clear and pristine streams, which offer excellent fishing opportunities for native Apache trout. Anglers can cast their lines into the cool, running waters while surrounded by the serene beauty of the wilderness.

Camping in the Blue Range Primitive Area is a true backcountry experience, as there are no designated campgrounds or facilities. Visitors must practice Leave No Trace principles and be self-sufficient, as the area is intentionally kept primitive to preserve its natural character.

The solitude and tranquility of the Blue Range Primitive Area make it an ideal destination for those seeking a genuine wilderness experience. It's a place where the rhythms of nature are undisturbed, and visitors can reconnect with the wilderness and experience the beauty of untouched landscapes.

23. Clifton and Morenci

Nestled in the rugged canyons of eastern Arizona, the twin towns of Clifton and Morenci offer a unique blend of history, industry, and natural beauty. Located in the heart of the Copper Corridor, these communities have a rich mining heritage and are surrounded by stunning landscapes that provide ample opportunities for outdoor adventures.

Morenci is home to one of the largest copper mines in North America, operated by Freeport-McMoRan. The massive open-pit mine is a testament to the importance of mining in the region's history and economy. Visitors can learn about the mining process and the significance of copper at the Morenci Mine overlook, where you'll be treated to a panoramic view of the immense pit.

Clifton, situated along the banks of the San Francisco River, boasts a well-preserved historic district with charming Victorian-era buildings. The town's history is closely tied to mining and the development of the region. The Greenlee County Historical Museum provides insights into the area's past, showcasing artifacts and exhibits that tell the story of Clifton, Morenci, and the surrounding communities.

Beyond its mining heritage, the region offers a wealth of outdoor recreation opportunities. The Coronado Trail Scenic Byway winds through the canyons and mountains, providing breathtaking vistas and access to hiking, camping, and wildlife viewing. The nearby Gila National Forest and Gila Box Riparian National Conservation Area offer additional opportunities for exploration.

The San Francisco River, which runs through both towns, is a popular spot for fishing and birdwatching. The area is a birdwatcher's paradise, with the chance to spot a variety of species, including the elegant Western bluebird and the striking vermilion flycatcher.

For those seeking a cultural experience, Clifton and Morenci host annual events and festivals that celebrate the area's history and culture. The Morenci Copper Classic Car Show, the Clifton Railroad Days, and the Clifton Blues and Arts Festival are just a few examples of the vibrant community events that take place throughout the year.

24. Roper Lake State Park

Roper Lake State Park, located in southeastern Arizona, is a hidden oasis in the desert landscape, offering a serene and refreshing escape for nature enthusiasts and outdoor adventurers. Nestled at the base of the majestic Mount Graham, the park is centered around a beautiful lake and provides a range of recreational activities, making it a popular destination for those seeking relaxation and outdoor exploration.

The centerpiece of Roper Lake State Park is a 32-acre lake that is ideal for boating, fishing, and swimming. The lake is stocked with a variety of fish, including rainbow trout, bass, and catfish, providing excellent opportunities for anglers of all skill levels. Visitors can rent paddleboats, canoes, and kayaks to explore the clear waters and enjoy the tranquil surroundings.

The park features a sandy swimming beach with designated swimming areas, making it a family-friendly spot for cooling off during the hot Arizona summers. Picnic areas with shaded ramadas and barbecue grills are available for visitors to enjoy lakeside picnics and gatherings.

Roper Lake State Park offers a range of camping options, from tent sites to RV sites with full hook-ups. Camping at the park allows guests to fully immerse themselves in the natural beauty of the area, and many campers wake up to stunning sunrise views over the lake.

Hiking enthusiasts can explore the park's scenic trails, which wind through the surrounding desert terrain and offer opportunities for birdwatching and wildlife viewing. The park is home to a diverse range of bird species, making it a popular destination for birdwatchers. Waterfowl, shorebirds, and migratory birds can often be spotted around the lake.

The park's location near the Pinaleno Mountains (Mount Graham) allows for stunning stargazing opportunities. The park frequently hosts astronomy programs, where visitors can observe the night sky through telescopes and learn about the celestial wonders above.

For those interested in the local flora and fauna, the park's Discovery Center provides educational exhibits and information about the natural history of the area.

25. Mount Graham International Observatory

Mount Graham, located in southeastern Arizona, is home to one of the most unique and significant astronomical observatories in the world, the Mount Graham International Observatory (MGIO). Perched at an elevation of over 10,000 feet, this observatory offers astronomers unparalleled access to the cosmos and is renowned for its groundbreaking research and contributions to our understanding of the universe.

The observatory is situated on Mount Graham, one of the "Sky Islands" of the Sonoran Desert, known for its exceptionally clear and stable atmospheric conditions. These conditions, coupled with the high elevation, make Mount Graham an ideal location for observing celestial objects. The MGIO is equipped with multiple telescopes, including the Large Binocular Telescope (LBT), which boasts the world's most advanced optical and infrared instruments. The LBT is a binocular telescope, featuring two massive 8.4-meter mirrors that work in tandem to capture stunningly detailed images of distant galaxies, nebulae, and stars.

Another notable telescope at the MGIO is the Vatican Advanced Technology Telescope (VATT), operated by the Vatican Observatory. This telescope is dedicated to conducting research in astrophysics and planetary science, contributing to our understanding of the solar system and beyond.

In addition to the cutting-edge research conducted at the MGIO, the site also offers educational programs and public outreach events. Visitors can learn about the observatory's scientific endeavors, explore the universe through guided tours and lectures, and even observe celestial objects through powerful telescopes.

The Mount Graham International Observatory is also home to a variety of native wildlife and plant species, as the mountain is part of the Coronado National Forest. Visitors can appreciate the natural beauty of the Sky Island ecosystem and explore hiking trails that wind through the mountain's lush forests.

The observatory is not without controversy, as its location on Mount Graham has raised concerns about its impact on the environment and sacred sites of the Apache people. Efforts have been made to balance scientific research with conservation and cultural preservation.

Western Arizona

1. Lake Mohave

Formed by the Davis Dam on the Colorado River, this 67-mile-long reservoir offers a tranquil oasis amidst the arid surroundings, attracting visitors with its stunning beauty and recreational opportunities.

Lake Mohave is renowned for its crystal-clear waters, which are ideal for a variety of water-based activities. Boating and fishing are particularly popular here, with anglers casting their lines in search of striped bass, largemouth bass, catfish, and other freshwater species. The lake's relatively calm waters make it a perfect destination for both experienced boaters and novices looking to cruise, water-ski, or jet-ski.

Many visitors take advantage of the numerous hiking trails that wind their way through the Mohave Desert, providing opportunities for exploration and wildlife observation. The area is home to a diverse range of desert creatures, including bighorn sheep, coyotes, and various species of birds.

Camping is another popular activity along the shores of Lake Mohave. The region boasts several campgrounds, some of which offer lakeside sites where campers can wake up to breathtaking sunrise views over the water. Whether you prefer tent camping or RV camping with full hook-ups, there are options to suit all preferences.

For those seeking a more leisurely experience, Lake Mohave offers several beaches where you can relax, swim, and soak up the sun. Katherine Landing, Princess Cove, and Cottonwood Cove are just a few of the beach areas where you can enjoy the lake's inviting waters and sandy shores. These spots are also great for picnics, family gatherings, and stargazing at night.

One of the unique features of Lake Mohave is its diverse underwater attractions. The lake is home to numerous submerged artifacts, including the remains of old mining equipment and boats. Scuba divers and snorkelers flock to the lake to explore these underwater wonders, adding an extra layer of adventure to the experience.

2. Black Mountains

The Black Mountains, a rugged and captivating mountain range in western Arizona, are a natural wonder that beckon adventurers, hikers, and nature enthusiasts. Stretching across the northwestern corner of the state, the Black Mountains are known for their stark beauty, rich geological history, and the sense of isolation they offer in the midst of the desert landscape.

The Black Mountains are part of the Basin and Range Province, a geological region characterized by alternating valleys and mountain ranges. These mountains have a unique appearance, with dark-colored, volcanic rocks that stand in stark contrast to the surrounding desert terrain. The most prominent peak in the range is Mount Perkins, which reaches an elevation of over 5,700 feet.

The Black Mountains offer numerous hiking opportunities for outdoor enthusiasts. Hikers can explore a network of trails that wind through the rugged terrain, providing access to scenic overlooks and panoramic views of the Colorado River and the surrounding desert. Popular hikes include the Mount Perkins Trail and the Cerbat Foothills Recreation Area, both of which offer a chance to immerse oneself in the beauty of the desert landscape.

Despite the challenging desert environment, the Black Mountains are home to a surprising variety of plant and animal species. Desert-adapted flora, such as cacti and Joshua trees, thrive in this arid landscape. Wildlife in the region includes desert bighorn sheep, mule deer, coyotes, and a range of bird species. Birdwatchers and nature photographers will find ample opportunities to observe and capture the diverse wildlife of the Black Mountains.

The Black Mountains have historical significance dating back to the days of early mining in the American Southwest. Cerbat, a mining town that once thrived in the region, played a crucial role in the area's history. Though the town is now a ghost town, its remnants can still be explored, providing a glimpse into the mining heritage of the Black Mountains.

One of the defining features of the Black Mountains is their remoteness. The mountains offer a sense of isolation and solitude that is often difficult to find in more heavily visited natural areas. he absence of large crowds makes it an ideal destination for those seeking tranquility and a connection with nature.

3. Route 66 Museum in Kingman

The Route 66 Museum in Kingman, stands as a captivating tribute to one of the most iconic and legendary highways in American history – Route 66. Situated in the heart of Kingman, a town that has long been associated with the Mother Road, this museum offers visitors a unique opportunity to step back in time and explore the rich history and cultural significance of this historic route.

The museum is housed in a beautifully restored Powerhouse building, which itself is a historical landmark. Upon entering the museum, visitors are greeted with an immersive experience that takes them on a journey through the heyday of Route 66. The exhibits showcase the evolution of this famous highway, from its inception in 1926 to its eventual decommissioning in the 1980s. It provides a comprehensive overview of the people, businesses, and communities that thrived along the route.

One of the museum's standout features is its collection of vintage automobiles, including classic cars and motorcycles, which take pride of place within its exhibits. These vehicles, some of which are meticulously restored to their former glory, serve as time capsules, transporting visitors back to the golden age of American road trips. The museum also houses a remarkable collection of memorabilia, signs, and artifacts, providing insight into the cultural and social aspects of Route 66.

A trip to the Route 66 Museum is not just about static displays. The museum offers interactive exhibits and engaging audio-visual presentations that allow visitors to gain a deeper understanding of the road's impact on American culture and its role in shaping the nation's identity. There's a sense of nostalgia in the air as visitors listen to the stories of the people who traveled along Route 66, from Dust Bowl migrants seeking a better life to adventurers on a cross-country journey.

Moreover, the museum is a valuable resource for those interested in the history of American transportation and infrastructure development. It sheds light on the challenges faced during the construction of the highway and its role as a vital link connecting the East and West coasts. Route 66 played a pivotal role in the economic development of many small towns along its path, and the museum highlights the various businesses that flourished as a result.

4. Kingman

Kingman is a historic and charming city located along the iconic Route 66 in the heart of the Mojave Desert. Known as the "Heart of Historic Route 66," Kingman serves as a gateway to many of the Southwest's most famous attractions and offers a perfect blend of rich history, classic Americana, and scenic beauty. With its vibrant heritage and welcoming atmosphere, Kingman has become a popular destination for road trippers and travelers exploring the legacy of America's Mother Road.

One of the top attractions in Kingman is the Route 66 Museum, located in the Powerhouse Visitor Center. This engaging museum takes visitors on a journey through the history of the famous highway, from the Dust Bowl migration to the heyday of American road trips. The museum features fascinating exhibits, vintage photographs, and restored vehicles that bring the spirit of Route 66 to life. The Visitor Center also provides information about the local area and serves as a hub for exploring Kingman and the surrounding region.

Kingman is home to a number of historic sites and classic roadside attractions that capture the nostalgia of Route 66. Visitors can stroll through the charming downtown area, where they'll find retro diners, antique shops, and beautifully preserved buildings, some of which date back to the early 20th century. Beale Street, the city's historic main street, is lined with unique shops and restaurants, perfect for a leisurely day of exploration.

Outdoor enthusiasts will appreciate the area's proximity to natural wonders, such as the Hualapai Mountains, which offer hiking, camping, and wildlife viewing opportunities. Additionally, Kingman's location makes it a convenient base for exploring nearby attractions like the Hoover Dam, Grand Canyon West, and the Colorado River.

Whether you're retracing the footsteps of travelers on Route 66, exploring the region's rich history, or enjoying the surrounding desert landscape, Kingman offers a warm welcome and a taste of classic Americana. It's a place where the past meets the present, inviting visitors to experience the enduring charm of Route 66 and the beauty of Arizona's high desert.

5. Oatman

Oatman is a quirky and captivating Old West mining town located along historic Route 66 in the Black Mountains of western Arizona. Known for its wild burros roaming the streets and its preserved Gold Rush-era charm, Oatman is a must-visit destination for travelers seeking a unique and unforgettable experience in the heart of the Mojave Desert.

Established in the early 1900s during a gold rush, Oatman quickly became a booming mining town, attracting prospectors and fortune seekers from across the country. At its peak, the town's mines produced millions of dollars' worth of gold, and the bustling community flourished. However, as the gold reserves dwindled, Oatman's population dwindled as well, leaving behind a near-ghost town. Today, Oatman thrives as a lively tourist destination that keeps its Wild West spirit alive.

One of the most charming aspects of Oatman is its resident burros, descendants of the pack animals used by miners over a century ago. These friendly burros now roam the town freely, greeting visitors and happily accepting snacks like carrots, which can be purchased from local vendors. The burros have become an iconic part of Oatman's identity, and interacting with them is a highlight for many visitors.

Oatman's historic downtown is lined with wooden storefronts, saloons, and shops selling everything from handmade crafts to Old West memorabilia. The Oatman Hotel, a landmark building that once hosted Hollywood stars like Clark Gable and Carole Lombard, still stands and is a great spot to grab a meal or enjoy the rustic ambiance. Daily gunfight reenactments take place in the street, adding to the Old West atmosphere and providing a fun, immersive experience for the whole family.

In addition to its Wild West charm, Oatman offers stunning views of the surrounding desert landscape and the winding, mountainous stretch of Route 66 that leads into town. The drive itself is an adventure, with hairpin turns and breathtaking vistas that make the journey to Oatman as memorable as the destination.

Oatman's blend of history, humor, and hospitality makes it a one-of-a-kind stop on Route 66, where the spirit of the Old West lives on and visitors can step back in time for a truly unique experience.

6. Topock Gorge

Topock Gorge, a hidden gem along the Colorado River in Arizona, is a haven for water enthusiasts and nature lovers alike. Located near the town of Lake Havasu City, this breathtaking gorge offers a unique blend of rugged desert landscapes and serene waterways, making it a popular destination for those seeking outdoor adventures and tranquility.

The primary attraction of Topock Gorge is its stunning waterway, formed by the Colorado River as it meanders through narrow canyons and past towering cliffs. The calm, emerald-green waters of the gorge are ideal for kayaking, paddleboarding, and boating. The surrounding cliffs and rock formations create a picturesque backdrop, making it a popular spot for photography and wildlife observation.

Boaters and paddlers can explore the scenic beauty of Topock Gorge while enjoying the serenity of the river. The gorge is also renowned for its hidden coves and beaches, where visitors can relax, swim, and soak up the sun. The clear water offers excellent opportunities for snorkeling and scuba diving, allowing you to discover the underwater world of the Colorado River.

Topock Gorge is rich in wildlife, with opportunities to spot desert bighorn sheep, waterfowl, and a variety of bird species. The area is part of the Havasu National Wildlife Refuge, providing a protected habitat for numerous species. Birdwatchers, in particular, will find Topock Gorge to be a rewarding destination.

For those seeking a more extended stay, camping is available along the banks of the Colorado River within the Havasu National Wildlife Refuge. The campgrounds offer a unique wilderness camping experience, with amenities such as picnic tables, fire rings, and vault toilets. It's an excellent way to immerse yourself in the natural beauty of the gorge and enjoy the solitude of the desert.

Exploring Topock Gorge is a tranquil and rejuvenating experience. Whether you're navigating the river's calm waters, hiking along its shores, or simply taking in the breathtaking vistas, the gorge provides a connection to the raw beauty of the American Southwest. It's a hidden paradise that invites visitors to unwind and appreciate the wonders of nature.

7. Lake Havasu City

Lake Havasu City, located in western Arizona along the Colorado River, is a vibrant and lively destination known for its stunning waterfront, outdoor recreation, and unique attractions. Founded in the 1960s by Robert P. McCulloch, Lake Havasu City has grown into a popular spot for boating, fishing, hiking, and exploring the desert landscape, attracting visitors year-round with its sunny weather and scenic beauty.

One of the city's most famous landmarks is the London Bridge, an iconic structure that was originally built in the 1830s and spanned the River Thames in London, England. In 1968, McCulloch purchased the bridge, had it dismantled and transported piece by piece to Lake Havasu City, where it was reconstructed over a canal on the lake. Today, the London Bridge serves as a unique focal point for the city, drawing tourists from around the world and providing a picturesque backdrop for shopping, dining, and sightseeing at the nearby English Village.

Lake Havasu itself is a paradise for water sports enthusiasts. The 45-mile-long lake is perfect for activities like boating, jet skiing, paddleboarding, and fishing, and its clear, blue waters are surrounded by rugged desert cliffs and sandy beaches. Popular spots on the lake include Copper Canyon, a favorite hangout for boaters and cliff jumpers, and the Bridgewater Channel, where visitors can enjoy the lively atmosphere as boats and watercraft cruise by. The city also hosts several annual events, such as the Lake Havasu Boat Show and the Desert Storm Poker Run, which bring excitement and energy to the area.

For those who prefer to stay on land, Lake Havasu City offers plenty of hiking and biking trails, including scenic routes through the surrounding desert and along the lake. The nearby Havasu National Wildlife Refuge provides opportunities for birdwatching and exploring Arizona's natural beauty.

With its mix of adventure, relaxation, and the charm of the London Bridge, Lake Havasu City is a unique desert oasis. It's a perfect destination for those looking to enjoy the outdoors, take in the stunning scenery, and experience the friendly, laid-back vibe of this lakeside community.

8. Sara Park (Special Activities and Recreation Area)

Sara Park, located in Lake Havasu City, is a versatile and vibrant recreational area that caters to a wide range of outdoor activities and leisure pursuits. Named after Sara Park, a community leader and philanthropist, this park offers residents and visitors a haven for relaxation, sports, and social gatherings.

One of the standout features of Sara Park is its extensive trail system, which is a paradise for hikers, mountain bikers, and equestrians. The trails wind through the park's diverse landscapes, including rugged desert terrain, rolling hills, and panoramic viewpoints. Whether you're looking for a leisurely stroll or a challenging hike, Sara Park has a trail for every level of outdoor enthusiast.

Sara Park is a popular destination for sports and recreation. The park boasts a variety of athletic fields and courts, including baseball fields, soccer fields, basketball courts, and tennis courts. These facilities provide opportunities for organized sports leagues, casual pick-up games, and sports enthusiasts looking to stay active.

For water enthusiasts, Sara Park offers access to Lake Havasu, a renowned destination for boating, fishing, and water sports. The park's boat launch ramp and fishing docks provide convenient access to the lake, making it easy for visitors to enjoy a day on the water. Whether you're into fishing, jet skiing, or simply cruising on the lake, Sara Park serves as a gateway to aquatic adventures.

Families and children are well catered to at Sara Park. The park features playgrounds, picnic areas, and open spaces for family gatherings and outdoor picnics. The expansive grassy areas offer a great place for kids to play, run, and fly kites.

Sara Park is also home to special events and community activities throughout the year. From outdoor concerts to festivals and community gatherings, the park serves as a hub for social and cultural events that bring the community together.

The park's natural beauty, with its sweeping views of the surrounding desert and nearby lake, adds to the overall appeal of Sara Park. It's a place where residents and visitors can escape the hustle and bustle of everyday life and immerse themselves in the serenity of the American Southwest.

9. Cattail Cove State Park

Cattail Cove State Park, located along the picturesque shores of Lake Havasu in western Arizona, is a serene and scenic destination ideal for nature lovers, water sports enthusiasts, and campers. Spanning 2,000 acres, the park offers a peaceful retreat from the hustle and bustle of everyday life, with breathtaking views of the lake and surrounding desert landscape.

One of the main attractions of Cattail Cove State Park is the access it provides to the crystal-clear waters of Lake Havasu. The park features a beautiful sandy beach and a designated swimming area, perfect for cooling off during Arizona's warm days. Boaters and anglers will also find plenty to enjoy, as the park has a convenient boat ramp and numerous fishing spots where you can catch bass, catfish, bluegill, and more. Whether you're kayaking along the tranquil shoreline, paddleboarding, or jet skiing across the lake, the park offers endless opportunities for fun on the water.

Cattail Cove State Park is also a haven for campers, with a well-maintained campground that features 61 campsites, many of which offer stunning views of Lake Havasu. The campsites are equipped with picnic tables, fire rings, and access to clean restrooms and showers, making it a comfortable spot to spend a weekend or a longer vacation. For those who prefer a more rugged experience, the park has several boat-in campsites accessible only by water, offering a secluded and immersive outdoor adventure.

For hikers, the park's trails wind through the rugged desert terrain, offering scenic vistas and the chance to spot native wildlife, such as bighorn sheep, coyotes, and a variety of bird species. The Ripley's Run Trail and the Whyte's Retreat Trail are popular routes that showcase the unique flora and fauna of the region.

Whether you're seeking a day of water sports, a peaceful evening under the stars, or a quiet hike through the desert, Cattail Cove State Park provides a perfect escape into nature. Its combination of lakefront beauty, outdoor activities, and a tranquil atmosphere makes it a favorite destination for visitors of all ages.

10. Parker Dam

Parker Dam, situated on the Colorado River near Parker, is not just an engineering marvel but also a critical piece of infrastructure that plays a vital role in water management and power generation in the American Southwest. This impressive structure offers visitors an opportunity to witness the intersection of human ingenuity and natural beauty.

Constructed in the 1930s as part of the larger Colorado River Aqueduct project, Parker Dam serves multiple purposes. First and foremost, it acts as a water storage and regulation facility, controlling the flow of the Colorado River and ensuring a consistent water supply for the region's agriculture and urban areas. The reservoir created by the dam, Lake Havasu, is a popular destination for boating, fishing, and water recreation.

Parker Dam also plays a pivotal role in generating electricity. The dam's hydroelectric plant harnesses the power of the Colorado River to produce clean energy for communities in Arizona and California. The juxtaposition of this modern energy production facility against the backdrop of the rugged desert landscape is a sight to behold.

Visitors to Parker Dam can take guided tours to learn about the dam's history, construction, and its role in water management and energy generation. The knowledgeable guides provide insights into the engineering challenges faced during its construction and the impact it has had on the region's development.

The location of Parker Dam offers stunning vistas of the surrounding desert and Lake Havasu. The adjacent Bill Williams River National Wildlife Refuge provides opportunities for birdwatching and wildlife observation, making it a haven for nature enthusiasts. The serene and picturesque surroundings make it a popular spot for picnicking and relaxation.

In conclusion, Parker Dam stands as a testament to human innovation and its ability to harness the power of nature for the benefit of society. It offers visitors not only a chance to appreciate its engineering prowess but also a serene escape into the beauty of the Colorado River and the surrounding desert landscape.

11. Bill Williams River National Wildlife Refuge

The Bill Williams River National Wildlife Refuge, located where the Bill Williams River meets Lake Havasu, is a hidden gem in the Arizona desert. Spanning approximately 6,105 acres, this refuge is a unique convergence of diverse ecosystems, including riparian, desert, and aquatic environments, creating a sanctuary for an extensive array of wildlife and plant species.

The refuge is named after the legendary mountain man, Bill Williams, and is a vital habitat for migratory birds, native fish, and various wildlife species. It's particularly important for the preservation of the southwestern willow flycatcher and the desert pupfish, both of which are endangered.

The riparian area along the Bill Williams River is one of the last of its kind in the Colorado River system. This lush environment stands in stark contrast to the surrounding desert, with towering cottonwood and willow trees providing a canopy for the rich undergrowth. This creates a green haven ideal for birdwatching, with over 355 bird species recorded in the area.

Hiking in the refuge is a remarkable experience, offering trails that meander through various habitats. The "Peninsula Trail" and the "Delta Loop Trail" are popular among visitors, providing scenic views and opportunities to spot wildlife in their natural habitat.

Fishing is another popular activity, with the river and nearby Lake Havasu offering excellent conditions for catching bass, catfish, and other species. Boating and kayaking along the river offer a peaceful way to explore the refuge and enjoy its serene beauty.

Photography enthusiasts and nature lovers are drawn to the refuge for its scenic landscapes and diverse wildlife. The juxtaposition of desert, river, and riparian environments creates a visually stunning setting, perfect for capturing the beauty of the Arizona wilderness.

12. Aubrey Peak Wilderness

Aubrey Peak Wilderness, located in the rugged and remote regions of northwestern Arizona, is a pristine and untouched wilderness area that beckons adventurers and nature lovers seeking solitude and breathtaking vistas. Covering over 15,000 acres, this wilderness offers a glimpse into the untamed beauty of the American Southwest.

The wilderness area is named after Aubrey Peak, a prominent summit that rises to an elevation of over 5,800 feet. Aubrey Peak and the surrounding terrain are part of the Mohave Mountains, characterized by rugged canyons, steep cliffs, and a diverse range of flora and fauna. The rugged landscape provides a challenge for hikers and backpackers, making it an ideal destination for those looking to test their wilderness skills.

Hiking in Aubrey Peak Wilderness offers a chance to explore remote and pristine desert landscapes. Trails wind through narrow canyons, leading to high ridges with panoramic views of the surrounding desert and mountain ranges. The area is known for its stunning wildflower displays in the spring, adding a burst of color to the arid terrain.

Wildlife enthusiasts will find plenty to see in Aubrey Peak Wilderness. The region is home to a variety of desert wildlife, including bighorn sheep, mule deer, coyotes, and a diverse range of bird species. Birdwatchers will delight in the opportunity to spot desert-adapted birds such as hawks, owls, and quail.

Camping in Aubrey Peak Wilderness is a primitive and rugged experience, with no designated campsites or facilities. Backpackers must carry in all their supplies and adhere to Leave No Trace principles to preserve the wilderness's pristine nature. Campers can choose to set up their tents in remote locations, offering a true wilderness experience under the starry desert skies.

Visiting Aubrey Peak Wilderness requires careful planning, as the remote location means limited access and services. Adequate water and supplies must be brought in, and hikers should be prepared for the challenges of the desert environment, including extreme temperatures and the possibility of encountering wildlife.

13. Alamo Lake State Park

Alamo Lake State Park is a hidden gem for outdoor enthusiasts, offering a stunning desert oasis surrounded by rugged wilderness. Nestled in a remote area along the Bill Williams River, Alamo Lake was created by the construction of Alamo Dam in 1968 and is now one of the premier fishing and camping destinations in the state. Its peaceful, scenic setting makes it an ideal spot for those looking to reconnect with nature and enjoy a wide range of outdoor activities.

One of the park's main attractions is Alamo Lake itself, which is known for its excellent fishing opportunities. Anglers flock to the lake for the chance to catch largemouth bass, crappie, catfish, and bluegill. The lake's healthy fish population and beautiful, uncrowded waters make it a top destination for fishing tournaments and casual anglers alike. Boating is also popular at Alamo Lake, with a boat ramp available for easy lake access. Visitors can spend the day exploring the lake by boat, kayak, or canoe, taking in the breathtaking desert views that surround the water.

Camping at Alamo Lake State Park is a favorite activity for many visitors, with campgrounds that offer a range of options, from primitive sites to RV sites with electric hookups. The park's remote location provides incredible opportunities for stargazing, as the lack of light pollution reveals a dazzling night sky filled with stars and constellations. Many campers are drawn to the park for the chance to experience the beauty and tranquility of the desert under the stars.

The park is also home to several hiking trails that wind through the desert landscape, providing opportunities to see local wildlife such as mule deer, wild burros, coyotes, and various bird species. Birdwatchers will appreciate the chance to spot bald eagles and other raptors that frequent the area, especially during the cooler months.

With its combination of excellent fishing, stunning scenery, and peaceful atmosphere, Alamo Lake State Park is a must-visit destination for anyone seeking a true desert escape. Whether you're fishing, camping, hiking, or simply enjoying the solitude, the park offers a memorable experience in one of Arizona's most beautiful natural settings.

14. Swansea Ghost Town

Swansea Ghost Town, nestled in the arid wilderness of western Arizona, is a hauntingly beautiful testament to the mining history of the American Southwest. This abandoned town, once a thriving hub of activity during the late 19th and early 20th centuries, now stands as a haunting relic of a bygone era.

The history of Swansea is intertwined with the mining industry, particularly the extraction of copper. Established in the late 1800s, the town prospered as miners flocked to the area in search of valuable minerals. The town boasted amenities like a post office, school, and saloons, catering to the needs of its growing population.

However, the fortunes of Swansea were closely tied to the ebb and flow of the mining industry. As the mines played out and the demand for copper fluctuated, the town's population dwindled. By the mid-20th century, Swansea was all but abandoned, leaving behind a ghost town that serves as a time capsule of the past.

Visitors to Swansea Ghost Town today can explore the remnants of this once-thriving community. Dilapidated buildings, rusting mining equipment, and crumbling walls stand as silent witnesses to the town's former glory. Walking through the empty streets, you can imagine the lives of the miners and their families who called this place home.

The town's remote location adds to its mystique. To reach Swansea, visitors must navigate rugged dirt roads, enhancing the sense of adventure and discovery. The surrounding desert landscape, with its stark beauty and distant mountains, creates a haunting backdrop for this ghostly relic.

Swansea Ghost Town is a destination for history buffs, photographers, and anyone intrigued by the idea of stepping back in time. It offers a glimpse into the challenges and triumphs of those who sought their fortunes in the harsh desert environment and serves as a poignant reminder of the impermanence of human endeavors.

15. Colorado River (Arizona Section)

The Colorado River, one of North America's most vital waterways, carves a dramatic and life-sustaining path through Arizona. Known for its breathtaking canyons, recreational opportunities, and historical significance, the Arizona section of the river is a defining feature of the Southwest.

In Arizona, the Colorado River serves as the boundary between Arizona and several neighboring states, including Nevada and California. Its journey through Arizona includes some of its most iconic landscapes, such as the Grand Canyon, one of the Seven Natural Wonders of the World. Over millions of years, the river has sculpted the canyon's towering walls, revealing layers of geological history and creating a spectacle that draws millions of visitors annually.

The river is also a critical water source in the arid region, supplying water to cities, farms, and communities across the Southwest. The Glen Canyon Dam, located near the town of Page, created Lake Powell, a massive reservoir that provides water storage, hydroelectric power, and recreational opportunities. Further downstream, the Hoover Dam forms Lake Mead, another significant reservoir serving Arizona and its neighbors.

The Colorado River is not only a natural marvel but also a hub for outdoor recreation. The river's rapids make it a world-class destination for whitewater rafting, especially within the Grand Canyon. Calm stretches of the river, such as those found near Glen Canyon, offer opportunities for kayaking, fishing, and paddleboarding. Scenic overlooks along the river's course provide awe-inspiring views and chances to experience the desert's beauty.

Culturally and historically, the Colorado River holds deep significance. Indigenous peoples, including the Havasupai, Hopi, and Navajo, have lived along its banks for centuries, relying on its waters and regarding it as sacred. Today, the river faces challenges due to overuse, drought, and climate change, prompting efforts to manage and conserve its resources.

The Colorado River in Arizona is a dynamic and essential part of the region, blending stunning natural beauty, recreational opportunities, and vital ecological and cultural importance. It continues to shape the landscapes and lives of those who depend on its waters.

16. Buckskin Mountain State Park

Buckskin Mountain State Park, located in the Parker Strip along the Colorado River, is a scenic wonder that combines the beauty of desert landscapes with the refreshing presence of the river. This park, encompassing approximately 1,677 acres, offers a diverse range of activities and breathtaking views, making it a favorite among outdoor enthusiasts.

The park's unique terrain features rocky mountainous areas, open desert plains, and the lush riverbank, offering a variety of landscapes to explore. Hiking trails in the park are a major draw, with paths like the Lightning Bolt Trail providing panoramic views of the Colorado River and the surrounding mountains. These trails cater to all skill levels, from leisurely walks to more challenging hikes.

Water-based activities are a central attraction at Buckskin Mountain State Park. The park's access to the Colorado River opens up opportunities for boating, water skiing, and swimming. The river's cool waters provide a refreshing respite from the desert heat, and the park's boat ramps and docks offer easy access for watercraft.

The park is also equipped with camping facilities, including RV sites and tent camping areas. These well-maintained sites allow visitors to stay amidst nature, with the convenience of amenities such as showers and picnic areas. The campsites offer a unique overnight experience under the starlit Arizona sky, accompanied by the gentle sound of the river.

For those interested in wildlife and nature photography, the park is a haven. The diverse habitats support an array of wildlife, including birds, reptiles, and mammals. Photographers can capture the interplay of light and landscape, especially during sunrise and sunset, when the desert and river are bathed in a golden hue.

Buckskin Mountain State Park is not just a destination; it's an experience that blends adventure, relaxation, and natural beauty. It's a place where the ruggedness of the Arizona desert meets the vitality of the Colorado River, offering a rich tapestry of experiences for all who visit.

17. Desert Bar (Nellie E Saloon)

Tucked away in the arid and rugged Arizona desert, the Desert Bar, also known as the Nellie E Saloon, stands as a unique and offbeat desert oasis. Located in the Buckskin Mountains near Parker, this one-of-a-kind establishment offers an unforgettable experience for those willing to venture off the beaten path.

The journey to the Desert Bar is an adventure in itself. Accessible only by rough dirt roads, visitors embark on a scenic drive through the desert, navigating dusty trails and rocky terrain. The remote location adds to the mystique of the destination, creating a sense of anticipation as you approach this hidden gem.

Upon arrival, the Desert Bar reveals itself as an open-air, Western-style saloon that appears to have sprung up from the desert floor. Surrounded by breathtaking desert landscapes, it's a place where old mining equipment, wagon wheels, and rusted relics blend seamlessly with the natural environment. The atmosphere exudes a rustic charm that harkens back to the days of the Wild West.

The Nellie E Saloon, named after the original miner's claim, serves as the centerpiece of the Desert Bar experience. Visitors can quench their thirst with a wide selection of beverages, including craft beers, cocktails, and non-alcoholic options. The menu features hearty, BBQ-style fare, making it a perfect spot to refuel after the challenging journey to reach it.

Live music and entertainment are regular features at the Desert Bar, enhancing the overall ambiance. Whether it's a local band strumming country tunes or a singer crooning classic rock hits, the music adds to the sense of community and celebration that defines the Desert Bar.

What sets the Desert Bar apart, however, is its commitment to sustainability. The entire facility is powered by solar panels, making it a shining example of eco-friendly practices in the desert. It's an unexpected sight in the midst of the arid landscape, highlighting the ingenuity and determination of those who built and maintain this unique establishment.

Visiting the Desert Bar is an experience that transcends a simple outing; it's an adventure filled with scenic beauty, a touch of history, and a sense of camaraderie among fellow travelers. It's a place where the desert landscape meets human creativity, resulting in a destination that leaves a lasting impression.

18. Parker

Parker, located along the Colorado River, is a vibrant and inviting town with a rich blend of cultural history and modern recreational activities. Known as the gateway to the Parker Strip, an 18-mile stretch of the river known for its beauty and leisure opportunities, Parker is a popular destination for water enthusiasts and those seeking a relaxed, riverfront lifestyle.

The Colorado River is central to life in Parker. It offers a playground for a variety of water sports, including boating, water skiing, and wakeboarding. The river's sandy beaches are perfect for sunbathing, picnics, and family gatherings. For fishing aficionados, the river provides abundant opportunities to catch bass, catfish, and carp.

Apart from the river, Parker is home to several cultural and historical attractions. The Colorado River Indian Tribes Museum offers insights into the heritage and traditions of the local Native American tribes, including the Mohave, Navajo, Hopi, and Chemehuevi peoples. This museum is an important destination for understanding the rich cultural tapestry of the area.

Outdoor adventures abound in the surrounding areas. Off-road enthusiasts will find the Parker area a haven, with numerous trails and open desert landscapes ideal for exploring by ATV or four-wheel drive vehicles. The nearby Buckskin Mountain State Park and River Island State Park offer additional opportunities for hiking, camping, and wildlife viewing.

Parker's community events, including boat races, fishing tournaments, and cultural festivals, contribute to its lively atmosphere. These events, along with local dining and shopping, offer a glimpse into the tight-knit community and the warm hospitality of this Arizona town.

19. Quartzsite

Quartzsite is a small desert town in La Paz County that transforms into a bustling hub during the winter months. Located at the intersection of Interstate 10 and U.S. Route 95, the town is surrounded by the striking Sonoran Desert landscape and boasts a fascinating blend of natural beauty, history, and unique cultural events.

Originally established in the 1860s as a mining camp called Tyson's Wells, Quartzsite has a rich history tied to the gold and silver mining boom. Its name reflects the abundance of quartz deposits in the area, which once attracted miners and prospectors. Today, the town is known for its vibrant rock and gem shows, making it a magnet for collectors, hobbyists, and enthusiasts from around the world.

Quartzsite's population swells from just a few thousand residents to over a million visitors annually during its peak season from January to March. The town hosts some of the largest gem, mineral, and fossil shows in the world, including the Quartzsite Rock & Mineral Show and the Quartzsite Sports, Vacation & RV Show. These events showcase everything from rare gemstones and fossils to handcrafted jewelry and outdoor equipment.

The town is also a haven for RV travelers and snowbirds, who flock to its vast open spaces and affordable camping options. Bureau of Land Management (BLM) land surrounding Quartzsite offers numerous areas for long-term camping, providing a serene desert experience under star-filled skies. The community's friendly and laid-back atmosphere makes it an appealing destination for retirees and adventurers alike.

Beyond the shows and camping, Quartzsite offers historical and outdoor attractions, such as Tyson's Well Stage Station Museum, which delves into the area's pioneer past, and the Hi Jolly Monument, a tribute to Hadji Ali, a camel driver who played a role in the U.S. Army's experimental Camel Corps.

Quartzsite is more than a stopover; it's a unique destination that combines desert charm, a vibrant community, and a treasure trove of geological wonders. Whether you're a rock hound, history buff, or RV enthusiast, this quirky Arizona town offers something special for everyone.

20. Wenden

Wenden, a small rural community located in western Arizona, is a testament to the charm of small-town America and the resilience of its residents. Nestled in the desert landscape, this unincorporated community offers a glimpse into a simpler way of life and serves as a gateway to the natural beauty of the surrounding region.

One of Wenden's notable characteristics is its close-knit and welcoming community. With a population of just a few hundred residents, Wenden exudes a friendly and neighborly atmosphere. Visitors passing through are often struck by the warm greetings and hospitality they encounter. The town's annual events, such as the Wenden BBQ and Rodeo, provide an opportunity for locals and visitors alike to come together and celebrate their shared love for the area.

While Wenden itself may not have a wide range of tourist attractions, its location is a treasure trove for outdoor enthusiasts. The nearby Alamo Lake State Park, situated about 30 miles to the northwest, offers a vast expanse of water for boating, fishing, and camping. Alamo Lake is renowned for its bass fishing, making it a popular destination for anglers seeking a quiet and productive spot to cast their lines.

For those interested in desert landscapes and wildlife, the region surrounding Wenden is a paradise waiting to be explored. The desert terrain is home to a variety of flora and fauna, including cacti, desert wildflowers, and numerous bird species. Hiking and off-roading are popular activities, allowing adventurers to immerse themselves in the natural beauty and solitude of the desert.

History buffs can also find points of interest in the area, with remnants of old mines and mining towns that tell the story of Arizona's mining heritage. The desert is dotted with abandoned structures, such as the Swansea Ghost Town, offering a glimpse into the past and the challenges faced by early settlers and miners.

Wenden's remote location and tranquil surroundings make it an ideal spot for stargazing and night sky photography. With minimal light pollution, the night sky above Wenden comes alive with a breathtaking display of stars and celestial wonders, making it a haven for astronomy enthusiasts.

21. El Dorado Hot Springs

El Dorado Hot Springs, nestled in the serene desert landscape of Tonopah, Arizona, offers a tranquil oasis away from the hustle and bustle of city life. This unique destination is a testament to the natural beauty and healing properties of the desert, providing visitors with a rare opportunity to immerse themselves in the rejuvenating waters of natural mineral hot springs. Located just west of Phoenix, El Dorado Hot Springs is a hidden gem within the vast Sonoran Desert, offering a peaceful retreat that taps into the ancient tradition of thermal bathing.

Upon arrival, guests are greeted by an environment that emphasizes simplicity and harmony with nature. The hot springs are part of a privately operated facility that has maintained a rustic and eco-friendly approach to relaxation and wellness. The water at El Dorado emerges from the earth at just the right temperature, rich in minerals that are believed to have therapeutic effects on the body and soul. The facility offers a variety of soaking options, from communal pools where guests can mingle and relax to private soaking areas that offer a secluded and intimate experience under the desert sky.

The layout of El Dorado Hot Springs encourages a connection with the natural world. Outdoor pools are set against the backdrop of the desert, allowing bathers to soak in the thermal waters while surrounded by the tranquil beauty of the Arizona landscape. Nighttime visits offer an unparalleled experience, with clear skies full of stars providing a magical canopy for those enjoying the warm waters.

El Dorado Hot Springs is not just about relaxation; it's also about sustainability and respect for the environment. The facility operates with a commitment to preserving the pristine nature of the desert, using eco-friendly practices to ensure that the springs remain a sustainable resource for generations to come. This approach extends to the use of solar power and the careful management of water resources, reflecting a deep understanding of the delicate balance of desert ecosystems.

Visitors to El Dorado Hot Springs can expect more than just a soak. They embark on a journey of relaxation, healing, and connection with the natural world. It's a place where the stresses of modern life are washed away by the mineral-rich waters, leaving guests refreshed, rejuvenated, and inspired by the beauty and simplicity of the desert. Whether seeking a solitary retreat or a communal experience, El Dorado offers a unique and memorable escape that embodies the spirit of the Arizona desert.

22. Kofa National Wildlife Refuge

Kofa National Wildlife Refuge, located in southwestern Arizona, is a sprawling 665,400-acre desert preserve that offers a haven for wildlife and a stunning escape for nature enthusiasts. Established in 1939 to protect the desert bighorn sheep, Kofa remains a vital conservation area and a showcase of Arizona's rugged desert beauty.

The refuge is named after the King of Arizona (Kofa) Mine, a gold mining operation active in the late 19th century. While mining once defined the region, today, Kofa is prized for its pristine wilderness and diverse ecosystems. It lies within the Sonoran Desert and features dramatic landscapes, including jagged mountain ranges, expansive desert plains, and seasonal washes.

One of the main highlights of Kofa is its role in preserving the desert bighorn sheep, a species that faced severe population declines due to hunting and habitat loss. The refuge's remote terrain and conservation efforts have helped stabilize their numbers, making it a prime location for wildlife observation. Other animals, such as mule deer, coyotes, desert tortoises, and numerous bird species, also call Kofa home.

Kofa's vegetation is equally remarkable, with iconic desert flora such as saguaro cacti, palo verde trees, and creosote bushes dotting the landscape. In the spring, wildflowers often blanket the desert floor, creating a vibrant display of color that attracts photographers and botanists alike.

Outdoor enthusiasts are drawn to Kofa for its solitude and opportunities for recreation. Hiking trails lead visitors through rugged canyons, up rocky peaks, and to historical sites like the remains of mining operations. The Palm Canyon Trail is a popular hike, offering a chance to see Arizona's only native palm species, the California fan palm, nestled in a secluded canyon.

Camping in Kofa is a rewarding experience, with numerous dispersed camping sites available. The lack of light pollution makes the refuge an excellent spot for stargazing, with clear views of the Milky Way and constellations.

Kofa National Wildlife Refuge is a testament to the resilience of the desert and its inhabitants, offering visitors a unique blend of natural beauty, wildlife conservation, and tranquil exploration in the heart of Arizona.

23. Castle Dome Mines Museum & Ghost Town

Castle Dome Mines Museum & Ghost Town, located near Yuma, Arizona, is a captivating destination that brings the Wild West to life. Nestled at the base of the rugged Castle Dome Mountains, this restored ghost town offers visitors an immersive journey into the region's rich mining history and the challenges of frontier life.

Castle Dome was once a bustling mining town, established in the 1860s during the silver and lead mining boom. At its peak, the area boasted over 300 mines, producing valuable minerals that fueled Arizona's development. However, as ore deposits dwindled, the town gradually declined, leaving behind abandoned structures and tales of a bygone era.

Today, the Castle Dome Mines Museum & Ghost Town preserves this history with over 50 restored buildings, many of which are original to the site. Visitors can explore saloons, blacksmith shops, general stores, schoolhouses, and miner cabins, all meticulously recreated to reflect their 19th-century appearances. Artifacts, tools, and personal items on display offer a vivid picture of the hardships and ingenuity of those who once lived here.

One of the most notable attractions is the mine shafts and tunnels, which provide a glimpse into the grueling work of mining. Guided tours take visitors through reconstructed sections, showcasing the techniques and equipment used by miners in the late 1800s. The museum also highlights the role of women and families in the town, adding depth to its historical narrative.

Surrounding the ghost town is the stunning desert landscape of the Castle Dome Mountains. The area offers hiking and photography opportunities, with trails leading to dramatic rock formations and panoramic views of the desert. The nearby Kofa National Wildlife Refuge adds to the appeal, providing a chance to spot local wildlife.

Castle Dome Mines Museum & Ghost Town is more than a historical site; it's a living tribute to the resilience and resourcefulness of Arizona's early pioneers. Whether you're a history enthusiast, a curious traveler, or a fan of the Old West, this hidden gem offers an unforgettable step back in time amidst the beauty of the Arizona desert.

24. Yuma Proving Ground Heritage Center

The Yuma Proving Ground Heritage Center, located in the vast desert expanse of southwestern Arizona, near the city of Yuma, stands as a monument to the ingenuity and dedication of the United States military's research and development efforts. This facility, part of the larger Yuma Proving Ground (YPG), one of the world's largest military testing sites, offers visitors an insightful glimpse into the history, technology, and operations of military testing and evaluation in the United States.

Spanning across a formidable landscape that provides the ideal backdrop for rigorous testing of military equipment under extreme conditions, YPG plays a critical role in ensuring that the equipment used by soldiers is reliable, effective, and capable of withstanding the harsh realities of combat. The Heritage Center serves as the educational and historical hub of this extensive testing facility, inviting the public to explore the technological advancements and strategic innovations developed here.

Upon entering the Heritage Center, visitors are greeted by an extensive collection of military artifacts, vehicles, and weaponry that have been tested on the grounds. From tanks and artillery pieces to smaller, yet equally vital, components of military gear, the exhibits cover a broad spectrum of military hardware. Each piece tells a story of development, testing, and refinement, highlighting the meticulous process of transforming concepts into combat-ready tools.

Interactive displays and informative panels guide visitors through the evolution of military technology, with a particular emphasis on the contributions made by YPG to advancements in warfare and defense strategies. The center not only chronicles the past but also offers a window into the future, showcasing emerging technologies and the next generation of military equipment currently under evaluation.

The Yuma Proving Ground Heritage Center is more than just a museum; it is a testament to the commitment of the United States to maintain a technological edge in defense and a tribute to the men and women who dedicate their lives to this mission. It educates the public on the importance of testing and evaluation in military readiness and honors the history of innovation that continues to protect and serve the nation.

25. Yuma

Yuma, Arizona, located in the southwestern corner of the state, is a thriving city with a rich blend of history, outdoor recreation, and cultural attractions. Known as the "Sunniest City on Earth," Yuma boasts over 300 days of sunshine annually, making it a year-round destination for visitors seeking warm weather and desert beauty.

Situated along the banks of the Colorado River, Yuma has a history that stretches back thousands of years. The area was originally home to Native American tribes, including the Quechan people, who utilized the river for sustenance and transportation. In the 18th century, Spanish explorers recognized Yuma's strategic location as a natural crossing point, and it later became a key stop for pioneers heading west during the 19th-century gold rush.

One of Yuma's most notable historical landmarks is the Yuma Territorial Prison State Historic Park, which operated as a prison from 1876 to 1909. Visitors can tour the preserved cells, learn about the lives of inmates, and explore exhibits detailing the prison's fascinating history. Another must-see is the Colorado River State Historic Park, where the Yuma Quartermaster Depot once served as a critical supply hub for frontier military outposts.

Today, Yuma offers a wide array of activities and attractions. The downtown area features charming shops, art galleries, and restaurants, along with seasonal events like the Yuma Art Center's festivals and farmers' markets. The Colorado River is a hub for outdoor recreation, including kayaking, paddleboarding, and fishing. Nearby, the Imperial Sand Dunes draw off-road enthusiasts and photographers to their stunning, otherworldly landscapes.

Agriculture is a cornerstone of Yuma's economy, earning it the title of "Winter Lettuce Capital of the World." The area produces a significant portion of the nation's leafy greens during the winter months, and visitors can experience farm-to-table dining or participate in agri-tours to learn about local farming practices.

With its unique history, sunny climate, and diverse activities, Yuma offers something for everyone. Whether exploring its historic roots, enjoying outdoor adventures, or savoring fresh local cuisine, Yuma stands as a vibrant oasis in Arizona's southwestern desert.

Made in the USA
Las Vegas, NV
11 March 2025